BTH

Rabia Siddique was born in Perth, WA, in 1971. After obtaining a Bachelor of Arts and Bachelor of Law degrees from the University of Western Australia, Rabia started her legal career as a criminal defence lawyer at the legal aid commissioner of Western Australia. In 1998 she moved to the United Kingdom with the intention of expanding her practise to the fields of International Humanitarian Law and International Criminal Law. In September 2001 Rabia was commissioned as a legal officer in the British army and served until 2008.

In 2006 she was awarded a Queen's Commendation for her humanitarian work in the Middle East and in 2009 was the Runner-up for Australian Woman of the Year in the UK. Rabia returned to Australia in 2011. She now works as a senior government lawyer currently based in Perth, where she lives with her husband and triplet sons. She is increasingly in demand as an inspirational speaker and story teller. Rabia is also in discussions about a UK/Australian feature film focusing on her life and the events in Iraq.

For more information on Rabia go to www.rabiasiddique. com.au

Rabia Siddique

EQUAL JUSTICE

MACMILLAN
Pan Macmillan Australia

Some of the people in this book have had their names changed to protect their identities.

First published 2013 in Macmillan by Pan Macmillan Australia Pty Limited
1 Market Street, Sydney

Cataloguing-in-Publication entry is available
from the National Library of Australia
http://catalogue.nla.gov.au

Typeset in Fairfield LH Light 12.5/17.5 pt Midland Typesetters
Printed by McPherson's Printing Group

Papers used by Pan Macmillan Australia Pty Ltd are natural, recyclable products made from
wood grown in sustainable forests. The manufacturing processes conform to the environmen-
tal regulations of the country of origin.

This book is dedicated to the four gorgeous 'men' in my life: Anthony, Noah, Oscar and Aaron, and is written in loving memory of my friends Charles Nathan 'Arnie' Arnison and Assaf Al Nahi.

CONTENTS

PROLOGUE

AL-JAMIAT

19 September 2005

I'm sitting inside a British Army Lynx helicopter as it begins circling the sprawling Hayaniyah district in the port city of Basra, in southern Iraq. I don't want to be here but it's my duty. I'm a major in the British Army; I've come to Basra to serve not just in the name of that army but also in the name of justice – to protect the human rights of the Iraqis who inhabit this land we have made our home, no matter how temporarily – and I've just been given an order to get in this helicopter bound for al-Jamiat, the notorious police station in this desperate city.

As the chopper swirls around, a frightening, chaotic scene is unfolding below us: hundreds of furious Iraqis are trying to storm the compound around al-Jamiat. The only thing

1

blocking their path is a cordon of British soldiers at the entrance. For these soldiers, the danger is obvious: many of the Iraqis have begun hurling petrol bombs, and black smoke is filling the sky above the compound. The violence is doubly alarming as there's a real possibility that Shiite militants in the crowd may begin firing rocket-propelled grenades at the foreign troops they so hate.

All this is taking place as the chopper brings us down, its blades cutting ribbons through the smoke. I'm afraid of what awaits us here, among these men who want us gone so badly – but I'm also here to do my job. There's no room for fear, not even for doubt. For now, the mission is what matters.

I'm in Basra as the sole legal adviser to the UK brigade commander in Iraq, but what's put me in this helicopter is that it has fallen to me – a 33-year-old, Australian-born military lawyer from a Muslim background – to help save the lives of two British Special Forces soldiers who are being illegally held captive somewhere inside the police station compound.

So here I am, wearing full-body armour and cradling an SA80 assault rifle between my knees. I have a moment to wonder whether many other military lawyers have found themselves so far out of their comfort zone, rescuing SAS soldiers from Islamic extremists. It certainly wasn't part of my job description when I joined the army as a lawyer, looking for something different from the routine of law firms, client meetings and court visits. I joined because being a lawyer in the army afforded me the opportunity to practise law in a way that had meaning for me. In Basra, that has meant acting on behalf of Iraqi citizens. Right now, it means heading into a situation with a completely unpredictable outcome.

The Jamiat police station is an extremely dangerous place for any member of the British Army, let alone our two SAS soldiers. It's the headquarters of the Serious Crimes Unit (SCU), which local Iraqis refer to – without joking – as the 'Murder Squad'.

They know, and we know, that the SCU is staffed and run by members of a Shiite insurgency group called Jaish al-Mahdi, which was set up a couple of years ago by the notorious anti-occupation cleric Muqtada al-Sadr. The SCU really are the bad guys. By day, they masquerade as police officers; by night, they kidnap, torture and murder Sunnis, foreign civilians and soldiers, as well as liberal members of the Iraqi community who refuse to be told what to do by the Islamic fundamentalists trying to invade all forms of government in southern Iraq. The British have controlled southern Iraq – and Basra – since the 2003 invasion, when Saddam Hussein was overthrown, but the infiltration of the city's police force by Jaish al-Mahdi insurgents has put everyone's lives at risk.

The police officer who essentially runs the SCU is a man called Captain Jaffar. We have good intelligence that Jaffar is a senior member of Jaish al-Mahdi and, accordingly, his house has become the focus of a covert surveillance operation. The two SAS soldiers were involved in this operation when they aroused the suspicions of local Iraqis, who noticed the two strangers – dressed in civilian clothing and wearing *shemaghs*, or Arab scarves, around their faces – driving around in a car and taking photographs. The locals alerted the police, who set up a checkpoint to intercept the pair, but when the soldiers spotted the checkpoint they opened fire, reportedly seriously injuring one of the policemen.

The soldiers took off as fast as they could, but didn't get far before their car was surrounded by Iraqi police, who forced them to a halt. The soldiers, whom I'd met and knew by their pseudonyms as Ed and Di, immediately identified themselves as members of the British military. At this point they should have been handed over to the British military occupation authorities, as required under the Status of Forces Agreement between the British and Iraqi governments. Instead, the police clubbed them with rifle butts and took them directly to the Jamiat – apparently on Jaffar's orders, after his men had contacted him and alerted him to the incident.

When we heard what had happened, back at our base at Basra Airport, we feared the worst. Only two days earlier, British and Iraqi troops had arrested and detained a man called Ahmed al-Fartusi, who we knew was the head of the southern Iraq arm of Jaish al-Mahdi. If the condition for letting Ed and Di go was Fartusi's release – as we suspected it might be – then we were all in very big trouble.

So the news was grim even before an update came through a short time later, about rumours being spread throughout the city: that the strangers arrested by the police were, in fact, Israeli spies. This is just about the worst thing that anyone could allege about our two soldiers. Iraq and Israel are not friends and never have been. Just as they were meant to, the rumours sparked huge anger and brought hundreds of enraged Iraqis to the entrance of the police station, where they are now watching our arrival.

As soon as we learnt the soldiers were in the Jamiat, the head of the UK brigade's surveillance unit, Major James Woodham, was sent to try to persuade the police to release them. By the time he was allowed to see them, they were bloodied, blindfolded and chained to chairs in a cell. But his negotiations to have the pair freed went nowhere.

The police at the Jamiat, as well as an Iraqi judge who's been summoned to the station, have told James they won't speak to anyone except 'Major Rabia', as they call me. I've often been to the Jamiat as part of my job with the army. I know some of the police there quite well, and I also know the judge in question, Raghib al-Mudhaffar, who works for the chief judge of Basra, Laith Abdul Sammad, known by us as Judge Laith.

Indeed, I've often gone 'outside the wire' in both Basra and Baghdad to give the Iraqi judiciary and other law enforcement agencies as much help as they need to re-establish the rule of law in their region. I've done this because although it's not technically part of my job, I feel it's part of my role. We're in this place to help the local people – and, yes, even lawyers can help people. Returning stability to this region is crucial, and the rule of law is vital to that stability. Accordingly, I've done whatever I can to help bring this about.

So I know a lot of key Iraqi officials, and my hope is that my Muslim background, as well as the respect I've always shown them and my ability to speak a little Arabic, have helped break down barriers. We're regarded as an occupying army and it has been important for me to gain their trust. I haven't done this cynically; I've genuinely wanted to form relationships with these people. It is, as I've learnt in the past, the only way we can work together effectively.

Since I've arrived here I've often been asked about my background, and I've replied that I was born in Perth, Australia, and grew up there – the elder child of a Muslim Indian father and a Protestant Australian mother who converted to Islam when she got married. What the Iraqis have made of this I don't know, but they seem to accept me and I've therefore felt I can do my work effectively.

That work has often involved visits to al-Jamiat. After I was posted to Basra, one of my highest priorities became the preparation of a class action for the Iraq Central Criminal Court in Baghdad against certain members of the Iraqi Police Service. These were men who'd allegedly tortured and murdered more than 300 Sunni Iraqis in Basra alone, during the two years since the 2003 invasion. When I first started visiting al-Jamiat, more than 200 local Sunni men and boys were being illegally held there, many without charge, in appalling conditions.

So in one way James Woodham's urgent message – relaying the requests from the police and Judge Raghib that I be sent to the Jamiat as quickly as possible – is understandable. They know me. But they also know James – he has accompanied me several times when I've gone to the police station to carry out human rights monitoring of prisoners – so on the face of it there is no clear reason why they've requested my presence in addition to his. When the message came, however, it wasn't the time to try to work out the politics at play over at the police station. Our chief of staff, Major Rupert Jones, ordered me to get in a chopper and go.

I was concerned enough by this order to phone the brigade commander, Brigadier John Lorimer, who instructed me to stay at the base. He thought the situation too volatile. I haven't been trained for close combat and I'm not a trained hostage negotiator. Rupert, however, countermanded this order. Rank was no obstacle to him; he'd often butt back against full colonels and lieutenant colonels despite the fact he was only a major. His father, Lieutenant Colonel 'H' Jones, was killed in the Falklands War while Rupert and his brother were still young, and afterwards had been celebrated as a hero. So Rupert had big shoes to fill.

'Do your fucking job. Go in there and get those boys out,' he said when I informed him of Brigadier Lorimer's order. Or words to that effect.

That's all very well, but hostage negotiation is not part of my job – and this thought was very much on my mind as I left on that chopper for the Jamiat. Hostage negotiation requires skills not covered in law degrees, not even in the sort of law practice I have here in Basra. But I will follow my orders.

Once we begin circling the police station, it's obvious things are much worse than I was told back at base. My sense of foreboding – so easily triggered in this sort of situation – is growing with each turn of the rotor. Iraqi police officers have positioned themselves on the roofs of some of the compound's buildings, with their weapons ostensibly pointed at the Iraqi protestors. In reality, they're aiming them at the British soldiers guarding the entrance.

As the chopper goes into a combat descent – straight down very fast – I feel fear and real doubt that I have the ability to negotiate a hostage release. I'm also terrified at the thought of having to use my assault rifle for real, for the first time. Before we land I try to find faith, to force myself to believe that God will look after me and provide me with the strength and wisdom to do what is needed. This is not some moment-of-crisis conversion – my faith in a being greater than us all is real; I just don't call on it too often.

This is probably also the moment when I realise that in the rush to get to the Jamiat, I've forgotten to put on the hijab I've always worn as a mark of respect when working in my official role with Iraqis, most of whom are men. Although not a garment I was in the habit of wearing regularly, it's a part of Iraqi culture. But obviously there's nothing I can do about my missing hijab now.

The chopper lands for safety's sake a short distance from the police station, and I spend those last few moments of relative peace preparing myself psychologically for whatever is about to happen. By now I can see a number of British tanks on the outer perimeter of the compound. The crowd is screaming abuse. Explosions from petrol bombs being lobbed by members of that crowd are becoming more frequent, and the sound of small-arms fire is everywhere.

I run from the chopper as fast as I can, so the pilot can immediately take off again – it's not safe for him to stay. For one weak moment I feel panic, but then within two or three seconds I tense up physically as I get ready – not necessarily for action, but to go into al-Jamiat and get Ed and Di out. And very quickly I say a prayer in my head: *Dear God, give me the strength and the wisdom and the courage to do what I need to do, and keep me safe.*

Two British officers arrive and we drive in a Land Rover towards the gates of the compound, but we have to stop about 100 metres away because by now the crowd is so big we can't get through it. At this stage one of the officers from the Coldstream Guards – the regiment keeping the Iraqi protestors at bay – escorts me almost to the front entrance of the station. Here, a couple of armed Iraqis – possibly police – part the crowd and allow me to enter the compound. This, however, infuriates the rioters. There's a lot of screaming and shouting, and abusive Arabic words directed at me; it's nerve-racking.

James appears, looking tense. He's been separated from the men in his unit. They arrived at the Jamiat with him but weren't allowed into the compound. A British military interpreter accompanying James turns white the moment he sees me.

'Sorry, sir, I can't do this,' he says and then basically runs out of the compound with his hands over his head. I guess he's either very ill or finds this to be the last straw: sending a woman into the situation.

'Thank you for coming,' James says. 'It's good you're here.'

At least he's staying. The next moment, the gates close behind us.

The police station is divided into two compounds: the so-called Serious Crimes Unit operates in one; in the other another section of the Iraqi police, the Department of Internal Affairs (DIA), is headquartered. We've always been less interested in the DIA because their officers are pretty much controlled by the SCU, but we've had more success dealing with the DIA than the SCU, and found them more cooperative – although none of the men from either unit is to be trusted.

James and I now go directly to see Colonel Ali al-Sewan, head of the DIA. We find the colonel sitting at his desk, flanked by a number of his police officers, whom I've seen before in meetings. Also present are probably half a dozen SCU men, some of whom we know to be members of Jaish al-Mahdi. Whenever I've visited the Jamiat in the past, the SCU men have always remained at a distance – but that certainly isn't the case today. The room is far too small for any of us to keep a distance.

Judge Raghib is also there. Everyone calls him 'the terrorist judge' because he presides over the terrorist court – although for the Iraqis the word 'terrorism' includes a gamut of offences those in the West would classify very differently. Any act seen as being against the radical fundamentalist regime in southern Iraq is branded as terrorism. Consequently, most of the more serious crimes end up before Judge Raghib.

The intriguing thing about Judge Raghib's request for me to be sent to al-Jamiat is that I don't entirely trust him. From information and also from my own research, he doesn't seem to be playing a very straight game at all. I've been concerned about the way he deals – or, in some cases, doesn't deal – with people in detention. Moreover, I've only just started working with him and I don't think we have built up such a strong relationship.

I've been quite robust with him on occasion because he has had a lot to answer for in terms of delaying the court process, not dispensing justice and not giving people the opportunity to face their charges. These aren't things I'm prepared to ignore, no matter who I'm dealing with. Maybe he has formed an impression of me in these few dealings we've had. Maybe he's been advised – by someone whose identity I can't guess – that he is to negotiate only with me. Maybe it's a bit of both. It's puzzling, though.

The others in the room include, predictably, a number of Shiite clerics. Saddam Hussein's regime was run mainly by Sunni Muslims until they were overthrown by the Shiites after the allied invasion of Iraq.

So this is the mix James and I are dealing with, and it's not encouraging: Shiite clerics, senior police officers who are really extremists and insurgents – and one other figure. For standing next to Colonel Sewan is Captain Jaffar.

Typically, business meetings in Basra start with half an hour of small talk and pleasantries. In other circumstances, we would be offered a soft drink at this point, but this time – significantly – we're not offered anything. There seems to be a lot of discussion going on between the policemen and the clerics, although I can't understand what's being said because they're talking in low voices. The clerics did a double take when I first walked in with James, no doubt because they're

11

not used to seeing me without a hijab, but at this stage I'm still being treated professionally, and with respect, by the Iraqi men in the room.

James and I have a volunteer interpreter with us; he's not fluent in English, but he's good enough. When I feel it's safe to proceed – and using the respectful, rather grandiose way of speaking that is common at meetings with Iraqis – I say, 'You've asked for me. I've come willingly. I've come with pleasure. I believe there has been a misunderstanding.' I go on to say that I'm here to clear up this misunderstanding, and I ask if it's possible to see the two prisoners before we get down to business.

Both Colonel Sewan and Captain Jaffar try to speak at this point, but Judge Raghib puts up a hand as if to say, 'No, I'm running the show.' From there on, for the next ten minutes, the conversation is pretty much between the judge and me.

'You know these men have done terrible things,' Judge Raghib says. 'I've heard they shot civilians. They're spies. I don't think they're British.'

'I have very good information that they really are British soldiers,' I tell him. 'In regard to what they've done, let's talk about that later. But you can trust me. You know me. If they've done anything wrong, I will see to it that justice is served.'

I then remind him about the law, which states that the Iraqis must hand the two prisoners over to us, and reiterate that he knows I'm a person of my word and that I'll do the right thing. 'We can keep having this conversation,' I add, 'but first, please, may I see the two men? I'd like to see for myself they're all right.'

Judge Raghib says something to the colonel. Their discussion looks heated, but the judge gets his way.

I'm slowly starting to feel that I have a little bit of power in this situation. The judge and I appear to be making headway, and I feel we're definitely on our way to brokering a deal. No one else has been part of our discussion – neither the clerics nor the other police officers. I don't, though, find anything strange in this – the judge and I are conducting a negotiation, and negotiations are usually simpler when they involve only two people. Eventually, we all stand up to walk over to the adjacent compound where the SAS men are being held, but James is told to sit down – they won't allow him to come with me.

'I'm not going without him,' I say immediately – because all the clerics and the police officers have stood up at the same time. There's no way I'm going to be taken to another compound accompanied by about twenty of these guys – most of whom I don't trust – and be separated from my only colleague and ally. Nor is it safe for him to be left behind without *his* only ally. We have to stay together. 'Major James is coming with me,' I reiterate firmly.

I think how odd it is that my rifle hasn't been taken from me. James still has his, too. So we haven't been offered the usual cans of Coke, but we have been allowed to keep our rifles. Perhaps, with so many police in the room, our weapons were not considered a threat. Obviously, if James and I decide to make any attempt to use them, we'll be easy to kill.

Now, in the company of our warped version of a Praetorian Guard, James and I go out and around the front of one compound, then through the side door of the second. As we walk we feel the humid, dusty heat and pass portacabins just like the ones in our own compound. We see the sandy car park and the twin gates marking the entrance – and the barrier between us and the crowd outside.

I don't pay a lot of attention to what's going on outside the walls, although I can hear the noise of the crowd growing stronger and I also catch a glimpse of the tops of quite a few British tanks. They're a small reassurance that James and I are not alone. It is a reassurance I need, for by now I am fighting trepidation and anxiety by trying to focus on the job at hand.

I focus on the alleyways we have to walk through on our way into the second compound. These are flanked on both sides by SCU officers, whom I find incredibly intimidating, given their reputations as torturers and murderers. But I can't think about any of that for long. I'm here to do a job – and so is James – and we must do it. To allow myself to be distracted by fear is not useful. It's never useful.

We then walk up two flights of stairs to a concrete cell that's probably the size of a classroom, which is where we find Ed and Di – along with half a dozen policemen. Within seconds, another twenty or thirty police officers file in after us. The cell is suddenly crammed with people.

Ed and Di are lying on the floor. They're still hooded, handcuffed and in chains, although their hoods are taken off as we walk in. They both look at me; Ed gives me a little smile out of the corner of his mouth; Di just looks startled – perhaps I'm the last person he expected to see. I couldn't blame him – I'm the last person I expected to be here.

Both men's shirts are bloodied. Ed's head is encased in a bandage. They've both obviously been badly beaten. I ask no one in particular – but all of the officers in general – if Ed's and Di's handcuffs can be taken off and if they can be given chairs to sit on. I also ask for both to be given water. Their handcuffs are taken off without delay – a good sign, I feel – and they're given water.

'Are you all right?' I ask them both.

They nod, smile and say they are. I'm not allowed to talk to them too much – this is made clear by one of the officers in the room – but I do tell them that everything is going to be fine and that we'll get them out of there. By now, though, there's so much noise from the crowds outside the station that I can't be sure how much they've heard.

Chairs are brought for the men, and one for me as well. A fourth chair is brought for the judge. No one else is given a seat. No one else seems to be a player at this point. But the police in the cell are standing very, very close to me. It's clear that they mean to intimidate me. I'm determined not to let them.

'Thank you for letting me see our soldiers,' I say to Judge Raghib in Arabic, picking up our conversation. 'Can we have a discussion in their presence?'

'I don't see why not,' the judge replies.

We discuss the conditions the judge would be happy to sign off on if Ed and Di are to be released into my custody; the translator writes these down as part of a rough document. In essence, these conditions are that the Iraqi investigators will be allowed access to the soldiers, to interview them, and I will ensure an independent investigation on our side.

The two soldiers won't leave the jurisdiction until a full investigation has occurred, and if there's any evidence of wrongdoing or criminal acts on their part, they'll be dealt with. As to how they would be dealt with, we'll liaise with the Iraqis on this matter. But in the meantime they'll be released into my custody today. I also say I'll take evidence from Iraqis who've witnessed any wrongdoing.

The final term of the agreement is that by day's end a letter will be provided to the judge authorising the release of the two soldiers; it will be signed by either Chief Judge Laith or the governor of Basra, Mohammed al-Waili, who is also the head of Basra Provincial Council.

Judge Raghib agrees to all of this and I start to breathe out, just a little bit. The atmosphere in the room shifts slightly as we prepare to sign the document the translator has drawn up.

Suddenly, rocket-propelled grenades explode all around the building. The room shakes and I see flames shooting up outside. There can be only one conclusion: the compound is being stormed by the rampaging crowd. The officers inside the cell immediately start shouting. They grab Ed and Di, throw them in a corner, and handcuff and blindfold them again.

I stand up immediately. 'Stop! What are you doing?' I ask them. 'We just agreed to a set of conditions! You can't do this!'

There's more shouting in the cell – and then the police take the two men away.

'Stop! This isn't what we agreed!' I'm screaming in Arabic and English. 'Please bring them back, I beg you!'

The remaining police cock their weapons, grab me, grab James, and throw us out of the cell. Perhaps most terrifying of all for us is seeing Judge Raghib treated almost as roughly. It's not hard to guess what this means.

As the police surround us, Judge Raghib looks at me and says, in Arabic, 'I'm sorry. I no longer have the power. It's no longer up to me.' Then he walks away fast.

In this moment, there are many responses – physical and emotional – vying for supremacy inside me. The greatest is shock. We were so close to signing – to having Ed and Di released. I genuinely thought I'd brokered a deal and achieved what the army had sent me in to do. With Judge Raghib gone, my power is gone as well. I'm no longer in a position of control. Since arriving in Basra I've had occasion to feel nervous, concerned, worried and upset. Never before have I been scared. I'm scared now.

Aside from James, I have not a single ally present. I'm a foreign, female, Muslim member of the British Army in an Iraqi police station run by Shiite Muslim extremists who hate the occupying forces with a passion. Outside, a violent, vengeful crowd thinks we're trying to rescue two Israeli spies. I'm a stranger in a strange land. In the strangest of lands, perhaps. At the most trying of times.

James and I are forced back down the stairs and into a makeshift office, where Captain Jaffar and his men are waiting. We're surrounded by SCU officers – killers, every one of them. A large number of the hostile clerics who stood sullenly by as Judge Raghib and I talked are also present, together with a few civilians from the local community whom I've seen on other occasions. But there are no pleasantries or expressions of civility now.

The atmosphere has turned hostile – I can feel it, like daggers hovering in the air. There will be no negotiating Ed and Di's release with these people now. I don't know what's in store for us. These aren't the men I'm used to dealing with, and they're not used to dealing with me.

There are probably about forty people in the office altogether. I'm the only woman. A lot of men are sitting down, but just as many are standing up. James and I are also standing, and I begin to feel like an animal in the zoo. Everyone is staring at us, sneering and telling jokes under their breath, and looking at me in a very disrespectful way – any woman will know what I mean by that. This is especially frightening because of the conversations being directed at us, as well as the conversations going on between individual men.

I can understand what's being said: they're discussing whether they should kill us immediately or later on or take us to another location. Or maybe we should simply 'disappear', which basically means we'll be put in the back of a truck, driven to the middle of nowhere and shot in the back of the head. I repeat everything I hear to James, and we both steadfastly keep repeating the same phrases to our captors: 'We're not going anywhere,' we tell them. 'We refuse to go anywhere else.'

Then another group of men arrives and they seem to be in a frenzy. One of them – a stocky man with a short beard – screams over and over that the British forces have killed one of his relatives. So clearly *this* man knows we're not Israelis – but he also clearly knows we're from the British Army. And he's holding an AK-47 assault rifle. James stands just behind me, and there's a chair between us. I feel very vulnerable with my colleague at my back and nothing standing between me and that man.

Suddenly the screaming man cocks his weapon and points it straight at us.

For me, an old, familiar emotion comes rushing back. I'm alone. No one is going to protect me so it's up to me to take care of myself. The last time I felt this alone was long ago – when I was nine, and growing up in Australia.

CHAPTER ONE

EARLY DAYS AND LOST INNOCENCE

My parents met in the skies in the late 1960s.

My father, who is Indian, was a trainee pilot, but when he first set eyes on my white, Australian mother, he was the chief purser on her flight. Mum was a tour guide, and at the time she was taking a group of people through South-East Asia. From what I've been told, Mum and Dad had their first conversation somewhere between Hong Kong and Singapore, but that's about all I know of their first encounter.

My father learnt to fly with the Indian National Cadet Corps, which is part of the Indian military. He was seventeen or eighteen when he joined the corps, which trains cadets for the Indian Army, Navy and Air Force. In due course he was accepted by the air force as a pilot, but before he could begin work the march of history trampled all over his plans.

When India gained its independence from the rule of Great Britain, in 1947, it was divided into two separate states: one with a Muslim majority, which was Pakistan; and the other, India, with a Hindu majority. Following Partition, Dad's brother went off to live in Pakistan, as did many other Indian Muslims. Only days before my father was due to realise his dream and start work as a pilot, the air force suddenly deemed him a security risk and rescinded his commission. So despite having a Bachelor of Arts in English and geography, he made what I still believe was a peculiar decision and joined Air India as a purser.

I don't know very much about my father's family background, except that, like many Muslims in India, his ancestors were originally from Persia (modern-day Iran). His parents and grandparents were all born in India, and his parents both died very young. I always thought it was a shame that I never got the chance to meet my paternal grandparents. It would have helped me understand my father better and allowed me to learn more about my Indian and Muslim background. I know my grandparents' early deaths had a significant impact on my dad but we never discussed it, except for my father reminding me that I was named after his beloved mother. Rabia, in Arabic, means 'spring' – the season of new life and new beginnings; the season of my birth.

The family must have been quite well off three or four generations earlier, because my father's parents were traders of a sort: they owned shops and sent my father to a private school; his own father had been educated in the United Kingdom. My father eventually went into retail himself, in Australia, and had a successful career in management.

I think it was my great-grandfather who was sent to England for his education then returned to India accompanied by his white English wife. The story goes that the poor woman didn't make it out of the port once the ship had docked. My great-grandfather's relatives were lying in wait on the quay, and the minute he disembarked they paid his wife to return to England immediately. The joke in my father's family was that my own mother was the reincarnation of my great-grandfather's first wife. Perhaps that was how they explained my parents' marriage to themselves.

I don't know when my parents fell in love and decided they wanted to spend the rest of their lives together – it wasn't something they discussed or something I ever felt I could ask about – but it did seem that falling in love was the easy part. Having decided that he wanted to marry my mother, Dad then had to face the prejudice and intolerance of white Australia in the late 1960s and early 1970s – which were personified by my maternal grandmother.

Mum's mother came from a big, conservative, working-class family from Adelaide and she was very much a product of her era. Consequently, when my father asked for her blessing to propose to Mum, my grandmother was vile to him. She refused to accept my father, let alone countenance any thought of my parents becoming engaged, and even ordered her brother-in-law to have Dad run out of the country. Indeed, she went so far as to insist that her brother-in-law tell the Department of Immigration that this foreigner who'd suddenly appeared in their lives was an illegal immigrant, a criminal and guilty of more or less kidnapping my mother.

The message my grandmother's poor brother-in-law was ordered to give to my father included the threat that if Dad didn't leave the country – and leave my mother alone – they would make his life extremely difficult. I can only speculate as to how they planned to do that. My grandmother's plan fell apart as soon as the two men met and spoke at length. The man who was meant to send my father packing ended up feeling sorry for him, and expressed his sympathy for the predicament Dad was in. 'You clearly love my niece,' he said, or words to that effect. 'So follow your heart. Do what you need to do, son. You've put up with a lot from all of us.'

This man then tried very hard to talk my grandmother around, but without success: she flatly refused to accept my father. In the end, my parents eloped to Perth and married in a very low-key civil ceremony in 1970, with just a few friends around them. Then Dad took my mother back to India to live. The pair made their home in Bombay, as the city was called in those days, but when Mum became pregnant with me, they flew back to Perth, where Dad had arranged a posting for a few months, just before Mum was due to give birth so I could be born an Australian. So I was born in King Edward Hospital, Subiaco, in 1971 in the city where my parents married, and was automatically granted Australian citizenship – just as they'd wanted. My first home was aircrew accommodation in Belmont, a working-class area near the airport.

Despite the past, though, my father didn't give up on my grandmother. After my birth, he sent her the first photo of me accompanied by a letter in which he wrote that he wanted to put everything in the past and very much wanted her to have a relationship with this new little granddaughter and her first grandchild. I think Dad's capacity for forgiveness and for reaching out to my grandmother, almost begging her to play a part in our lives, melted my grandmother's heart just a little. She must also have realised that she could only be part of my life if she accepted my parents' marriage. Funnily enough, within the first few years of my birth, my grandmother and Dad developed a very strong relationship to the point where, somewhat paradoxically, my grandmother ended up becoming really protective of him. Not surprisingly, it was around this time that my parents started calling me 'The Peacemaker'.

These family tensions weren't all one way, though – my father got a lot of grief from his own siblings in India when he and my mother married. Since my great-grandfather's abortive first marriage, Dad was the only man in the family to have married a white woman. In time, though, my birth became a uniting factor on his side of the family as well and his family would come to Bombay to visit us.

When I was five or six months old, my parents took me back to Bombay to live. Dad was still working for Air India and he was based there. Nanna had little to do with us then – our family relationship with her was only properly forged when we later returned to Perth.

I have vague memories of a very good life in a nice part of the city. We had a beautiful apartment and a servant called Rusalbi, a motherly figure I remember as probably being in her forties. I loved Rusalbi and spent a great deal of time with her. During the hottest months of the year we would sit and play for hours on the marble floor in the apartment. Rusalbi would talk to me in Hindi – I think she was the first person to teach me Hindi – and consequently I spoke Hindi before I spoke English.

Life in India wasn't so easy for my mother. This was a different era, and to be a white foreigner in Bombay in those days could be an alienating experience – just as, no doubt, it was for my father living in Perth. My parents had friends in Bombay, but Dad could be away for two or three weeks at a time depending on his flight schedule. It must have been challenging for a young woman from a completely different culture to be at home with her baby and a servant, with no friends to call on and a hostile set of in-laws.

If Dad went away for more than a month, though, we would usually go with him. Once, he took us on a posting to Beirut before the start of the Lebanese Civil War. We also travelled to cities in Europe and South-East Asia.

As time went on, my mother found living in Bombay more and more difficult and wearying. She'd become extremely homesick, which only made the trials of everyday domestic life harder to bear. Merely trying to buy simple provisions could be a complicated business, and India's political and economic instability didn't help. Two decades on from Partition, there was still rioting between Hindus and Muslims, and uprisings against the national government. White people were a particular target for any violence that was brewing.

These were no inconsiderable aggravations, which my father would have known. The result was probably predictable, especially once my parents started to consider my education: ultimately, they decided it would be best if we all moved back to Australia permanently. We left Bombay when I was five and, at that stage, still an only child.

Back in Perth, we lived first in the suburb of Belmont, in temporary aircrew accommodation. Compared to Bombay, Perth seemed small, quiet and clean. But it was a sunny, healthy, friendly place. My memories are mostly of going to kindergarten and crying a lot because everything was so strange. Until then I'd only ever been with my mother and father, and our servant and family friends, so I found kindergarten overwhelming. As well, I stuck out with my very good manners and strong English accent – although I, of course, thought the other children sounded strange. If that wasn't enough, I was a girl with dark skin, dark hair and big blue eyes among a crop of largely Anglo kids. Once we'd moved to a modest post-war home in Downey Drive, Manning – which was quite a working-class area in those days – I certainly had no more luck fitting in with the other children.

The house had two bedrooms and a lean-to out the back. Our street was made up of elderly, retired people, state housing and some indigenous families. We were one of only two Asian, mixed-race families on the street. My primary school was directly across the road, separated from our house by a large oval. At the end of our road was a strip of shops with a deli, fish-and-chip shop, barber, greengrocer and small supermarket, and a few minutes' bike ride away was my tennis club; I played a lot of tennis from the age of eight until I was fourteen. Our house was painted white with a red-tiled roof and low wall and three huge frangipani trees out the front.

Dad had realised he wouldn't be able to keep working in the airline industry if he lived in Australia. I don't think he could secure a job as ground staff for any other airline, but whether this was due to his race or a lack of available jobs at the time, I don't know. At any rate, he began looking for other employment. One of the first jobs he got was at Pizza Hut in Belmont. After kindergarten each day, he'd take me off to Pizza Hut, where I'd sit at one of the back tables with my crayons and drawing books while his staff kept an eye on me and fed me little ice-creams. I think they all felt a bit sorry for me because Mum was working pretty much full-time as a travel agent to help with family finances and Dad was working another job as well, as a security guard.

Even though he'd been very willing to move to Australia, life and his new circumstances must have been difficult for my father. I suspect it was something of a comedown for him to leave a comfortable, quite privileged life in India and work at two comparatively simple jobs in his new country while living in very modest accommodation in what must have seemed a backward kind of place: Perth in the early 1970s. At that time Perth was quiet, small and quite isolated from the rest of Australia. A small-town mentality pervaded: the residents clubbed together and didn't take well to outsiders. There were few foreigners – migrants, especially those who were either Muslims or Indians or both, were thin on the ground. So the Perth I knew as a child was nothing like the diverse, multicultural city it is today.

There weren't many dark-skinned people around then, but there was no real issue with us being Muslims at that time.

There was no war on terror, of course, no public discussion of what Islam means and what it does to people in countries where our soldiers die. We were just people with funny names. While we were still living in Belmont, however, some well-meaning people from the immigration authorities came to visit and offered Dad English lessons. This was amusing, given Dad had studied for an honours degree in English and geography back in India. He used to joke about it later on, so I think he took the offer with fairly good humour.

A lot less amusing were the frequent snide comments from strangers about his colour and his accent. People would make fun of his accent or say, 'I can't understand you,' when in fact he was very, very easy to understand. I remember going to the greengrocer's with him once and watching his frustration and humiliation as the greengrocer kept saying, slyly, 'I can't understand you, mate.' But Dad never revealed his true feelings in public. He'd face things with great humour, make fun of himself, and was always smiling and charming. Never, ever would he let on to people that their racism was breaking his heart.

As I grew old enough to work out what was happening, I wanted to shout at these people that my father was an educated man who'd lived and travelled all over the world. This treatment of my father seemed to me an injustice – and injustices have never sat well with me, from a young age. Of course, as a child I was limited in what I could do to redress this particular injustice – and I never did shout at anyone – but I felt, keenly, that something was not right and also felt how strongly I wanted to make it right. What I witnessed made me feel sad as well. I was sad for my father, and also sad that people could be so ignorant and nasty. I think this was my first experience of sadness.

Clearly, because of my mother – and for the sake of my future – my dad was willing to make the sacrifice he did and live in a culture that wasn't his own and tolerate being treated as 'a foreigner'. I understood this and appreciated him for it. All the same, like many children of migrants, I was mindful from a young age that I ought to do really well at school and later on at university to make their sacrifice worthwhile. It was a bit of a burden, but even at the time I was genuinely grateful to my dad that he was working so hard to make a life for us.

There's no doubt that those first few years of living in Australia left a permanent mark on my father. He came to believe that because he was a foreigner, and a Muslim, he'd only go so far in his career. The proof of this, as he saw it, came after he moved into retail management and was passed over for promotion by his employers, even though he was clearly the most suitable candidate. He started teaching me that his differentness had disqualified him, although I also remember hearing him expressing frustration at how ignorant and small-minded people could be. I can't remember whether he said this to me directly or whether I walked into a room and heard my parents talking about it, but it's a very strong memory.

With me, my father was both encouraging and damning. He'd say, 'Try your hardest to do your best,' before warning me there would always be obstacles in my path because I was different – because I wasn't like all the other Australians we could see living around us.

The frustration and anger he felt were clearly becoming a problem, because not long after his employer snubbed him my father had a stress-induced heart attack. He recovered, but it was an indication that Dad kept his strongest feelings hidden from us – to the point that it made him sick – and that we might never know what they were.

To me, being different meant I didn't have ham sandwiches at lunchtime when all the other kids seemed to. Because people knew nothing about Islam or Muslims when I was at primary school, that part of my background was never a problem for me, but this doesn't mean I wasn't teased mercilessly about a lot of other things, such as having olive skin.

The teasing about my English accent wasn't helped by a well-meaning teacher who made me stand in front of the class in my first week at primary school and recite 'The rain in Spain falls mainly on the plain'. 'This is how we should all speak,' she then announced to the children. I was teased for being clever, too, and by my second year in primary school I'd learnt not to put up my hand so much.

My name provoked the most laughter of all. The kids would call me Rabbit, Rabbi, Rabies or Radiator. Some of the bigger kids would call me Labia, although I didn't know what that meant until I was much older. I didn't find any of it funny. I hated my name and wished I had one people knew how to pronounce and didn't bring me so much negative attention. So when I was about six or seven I invented an alter ego, Caroline Jones, and I'd only answer to that name.

I wanted to be Caroline Jones, a blonde Catholic girl. My maternal grandmother was quite happy to feed my desire for a change of name. Even though she'd made peace with my father, perhaps she was still not entirely comfortable with some things about his background, and my name certainly did suggest our otherness. She called me Caroline for the next couple of years.

It was around this time that I started begging my parents for a brother or sister because I felt so lonely. My parents eventually granted my wish and in 1979 – when I was seven years old – my brother, Adam, was born. I was thrilled to have a sibling – I'd wanted him so desperately and now he was here. I absolutely loved this new little baby in our family and adored helping my mother care for him. There was nothing I wouldn't do for him, no amount of time I wasn't willing to spend with him. And there was something else: I was prepared to do anything – *anything* – to protect him. The fierceness of my love for him – the protective shape it took – would soon transform the path of my own life, for better and worse.

*

Next door to us in Perth lived a couple who must have been in their sixties. They'd both become close to my parents, and they were like surrogate grandparents to my brother and me. Nan and Poppa, as we called our neighbours, were practically part of the family. Poppa was retired, and he used to do some work in our garden to help my father out. The two men put a little swing gate at the back of our two properties so that Poppa had easy access to our house.

My parents both had to work full-time throughout each summer school holiday, which meant leaving me in charge of my younger brother. What I saw was my parents leaving us alone at home when I wanted them to stay home too, I just wished they could be around when *I* was around. I felt like I was the only child at school who dreaded the summer vacation, because although we did have fun and I loved my brother, I still had to look after him, and I was the kind of child to take that responsibility very seriously. Naturally, our parents told us not to go out, but we always knew that Nan and Poppa were next door if we needed anything. I can't remember now, but I'm sure I liked knowing they were close by. It would have reassured me.

One day during the holidays, when I was about nine and a half, Poppa came over to our house. He coaxed me to his side. I wasn't sure what he wanted, but I did as I was asked. He then started to fondle me, slipping his hand beneath my clothes and touching my private parts. When Poppa penetrated me with his fingers, I was far too scared to do anything. I had no idea about sex or boys – I was still interested in playing with dolls and riding my bike – so it wasn't as if I even related what he was doing to that. But I felt sick and knew instinctively, despite my innocence, that what he was doing to me wasn't right.

That was the start of the nightmare and a 'routine' that, to be blunt, destroyed my childhood and more besides. Poppa would usually come over and sexually abuse me while my parents were at work. Sometimes, though, when my parents would send my brother and me next door to play, Poppa would take advantage of this. He'd even orchestrate situations to get me on my own, either when my parents were next door or not around – and always when Nan was elsewhere.

It didn't take long for me to become one of those children who seems older than their years. Poppa was doing things to me that had absolutely no place in the life of a child. I'd been forced to grow up and, as is so often the case, not in the most pleasant of circumstances. Fairly soon I started having problems sleeping, and on occasion I'd wet the bed. I felt ashamed and thought that perhaps there was something wrong with me. But I don't think my parents suspected anything was really wrong. I think they just assumed wetting the bed was a normal part of childhood.

Right from the start, Poppa warned me never to tell Mum or Dad what he was doing and, like so many children before and since, I didn't. Poppa also said he'd quite like to have the same 'special time' with my brother – who was all of two years old then – before adding that he wouldn't need to do this as long as I kept making him happy.

Until this point I'd been coping with the abuse as best I could, on my own, with no mechanism to deal with it. But hearing that Poppa had designs on my brother devastated me. Adam was my precious brother. Anyone with a beloved younger sibling will understand how that feels. There was no way I could allow what was being done to me to be done to him. So I let Poppa carry on doing what he wanted to me, and the only thing that made it bearable was that I was saving Adam from the same fate. I could think of nothing else but my dread of Poppa, and the stress I experienced was extreme. My sleeping problems progressed to constant nightmares.

One day it all became too much for me. Poppa had come over to our house for some reason and cornered me in the back playroom. Through the window, I could see my brother riding his tricycle outside in the sunshine. Suddenly, I saw Poppa looking at him in exactly the same way he always looked at me.

How can I describe what I felt, as a nine-year-old, at that moment? My little brother was in terrible danger and our parents had left him in my care. If anything happened to him, it would be my fault. I knew right then that I had to tell my parents what was going on. Perhaps I worried about the consequences – Poppa had told me not to tell them, after all – but far worse was the prospect of what would happen if I *didn't* tell then. So, once Poppa left, I rang Mum. I think I broke down completely. I begged her to come home.

'Why do you want me to come home now? I'll come home after work,' she replied.

'You really need to come home now, Mummy. I really need to talk to you,' I said.

After some further persuasion, my mother came home and I told her the terrible secret I'd been living with.

My parents took me to see a doctor and I recall the examination being a bit painful. I distinctly remember wanting to go to the police because I was worried that Poppa might molest other children, and getting upset with my parents when they wouldn't let me. There seemed to be a lot of hushed conversations about how to deal with the situation. I was told not to speak to anyone at school about what had happened, including my teachers, and we were never to speak about the subject again. I seem to recall Nan being told about what had happened, but Poppa denied it, of course, and I think he tried to pass it off as something I'd made up or misunderstood.

My parents believed what I had told them about Poppa – but I felt that they just wanted the whole thing to go away. It seemed to me that my story, which they knew was the truth, was also something my parents did not want told – not even to them, and certainly not to anyone else.

It was the first time in my life when I felt truly powerless. I wasn't allowed to have a voice and I didn't understand why. These days I can see that my parents probably went into survival mode: they just didn't know how to deal with it and their response was to keep it quiet. At the time it happened, there was much less awareness of child sexual abuse than there is now, and child psychology wasn't really considered at all. There had been no church scandals. 'Kiddy fiddlers' were almost so unheard of as to be phantoms. Certainly, no one thought they came in the form of seemingly kind old men living next door with their wives.

I've tried to understand the context for that time, to understand my parents' reaction. I've tried to appreciate what society was like then, and I can see that maybe, as an unusual couple in a socially conservative country, they didn't want to 'make a fuss'. Perhaps they thought the police would behave differently towards them than towards a wholly Anglo family with the same story. Perhaps they thought the police would do nothing anyway. Perhaps they thought it would all be too traumatic for me. I was willing to go to the police, but perhaps they thought I didn't really know what I'd be letting myself in for. I don't know.

The abuse stopped, but the way it was all dealt with had the effect of making me feel abandoned to the consequences of what had happened to me. But I was only a child. I was *their* child. Something terribly wrong had been done to me. As far as I could tell, nothing was being done to right that wrong. My sense of justice – of what is right and what is wrong – had been clearly defined from so young an age that I can't remember not having it. To my mind, no justice was to be done. Poppa would never have to face the consequences of his actions, whereas I was living with them daily.

So I tried to find my own solution. I asked if we could move. We had an eat-in kitchen where we spent a lot of time as a family. The window faced the house next door, where Nan and Poppa lived. But we didn't move and so for the next five or six years, whenever I was at home, I'd pull the blind down in the kitchen so I wouldn't have to see Nan and Poppa. I'd also walk the long way around to and from school so as not to pass their house. It was a very small neighbourhood, though, and every now and then I would see them in the distance. I would duck and hide and do everything I could not to come face to face with them.

Poppa was no longer abusing me, but his influence on my life continued throughout that time. I was still organising my life around him. I didn't even get to have my neighbour-hood to myself, let alone my head with its many rushing, buzzing, overwhelming thoughts. In the end, when I was fourteen or fifteen, we moved away from Manning, but my childhood had effectively ended that summer.

We can never predict the repercussions of our actions far into the future. I couldn't know how the combination of events, decisions, actions and inaction of that time would ripple through my family's lives forever. If I'd known, though, I think I'd have stopped on the precipice of that summer and tried to take the measure of the crevasse I was about to fall into. It was a crevasse that separated me from my family, because at the point I fell they didn't reach in to pull me back – they stood on the edge and peered over to check I was not too badly damaged.

That crevasse was a place where love and justice and trust and belief seemed absent. I went in there on my own, and I can attest that it was cold and lonely. In many ways, I've been pulling myself out of it ever since – one foothold, one handgrip, at a time. It's been a long way up. But, as time has gone on, I've learnt how to climb.

CHAPTER TWO

CONTROL AND RESILIENCE

I wasn't brought up reading the Koran, and I didn't have a 'traditional' upbringing as the daughter of Muslims by any stretch of the imagination.

My mother – who was raised in a conservative Protestant family – converted to Islam after she married my father, but in a sense Dad distanced himself from his religion after we started living in Australia, and he decided not to bring it into the house. I think he made a conscious decision that the only way for the family to get ahead was if he, and we, did everything to fit in to our new country – for it was new for me as well as for him.

I identify as a Muslim because my father is a Muslim – and Islam, in a similar way to Judaism, is a birthright. 'Muslim', for me, is a way to define my cultural and ethnic background. Islam isn't a religion I practise – I have a spiritual practice, and I pray, not specifically to God, Allah or a prophet but to a higher power – this is probably as a result of the way Dad kept religion at a distance. He took me to the mosque once or twice soon after we arrived in Perth but after that we never worshipped anywhere. In a similar vein, although we did have some Muslim friends, we gradually spent less time with them.

Dad is a great thinker and he used to talk a lot about spiritual things, and about God and Allah, but we rarely discussed religions. As a result, my brother and I grew up without any formal religious education, although we were taught to believe in God and to live a good life. The only reminder that ours was a Muslim household was the absence of alcohol and pork.

My primary school in Manning was pretty rough. Luckily, I was a talented student, and my life improved dramatically when I was accepted as a student at Penrhos College, a fantastic private girls' school in Perth where I blossomed. A girls-only school worked well for me, because at that age I considered boys to be nothing but a pain. They certainly had been at primary school, anyway, when they always seemed to be trying to pull my dress up or to be playing the fool in class.

Penrhos was a wonderful, caring, accepting environment where I went from feeling alienated and 'different' to feeling unique and proud of my heritage and my 'exotic' name. I stopped grimacing every time someone called out 'Rabia!' and I stopped wanting desperately to fit in, because I *did* fit in. I worked hard, studied hard and threw myself into everything the school had to offer. I acted in plays, played sport and sang in the choir.

At the end of Year 11, I was nominated for school captain. When I came home and proudly told my parents the news, Dad said, 'Now listen, if you don't achieve this, it isn't your fault. Remember, you're the only Muslim. You're from a foreign background, you have a foreign name, and it would be a very brave thing for a Uniting Church school to allow you to become school captain.'

I respected my father and listened to what he said, but I refused to accept his appraisal of the situation. Perhaps my sense of self was already strong enough to know his words wouldn't necessarily apply to me, or perhaps I believed that balance and fairness existed in the world, or perhaps I was simply naïve. Whichever was the case, I was enormously moved when I went on to be elected captain. It topped off the first really happy chapter in my life: high school.

The highlight in my final year at Penrhos was meeting Queen Elizabeth II at a Commonwealth Youth Tea Party during her bicentenary visit to Perth in 1988. My parents were bowled over by this. They'd been proud enough of me already, but now I'd met the Queen! Even Dad came close to admitting he could have been wrong about my background and religion holding me back.

My relationship with my parents was good when I finished high school. Like all children, I wanted their love and approval, and to make them proud. As I came to the end of my secondary education, they *were* proud of me, just as they were when I was accepted into an arts degree at university. I'm still trying to work out what happened not long after I started at uni, when my relationship with both parents spectacularly and rapidly disintegrated.

Dad, it seemed, had trouble accepting that I'd become a young woman who could – and wanted to – make decisions about her own life. I don't think this had anything to do with his Muslim beliefs. I believe he was just so terrified for my safety that he didn't want me moving out of his sphere of control. What strikes me is this: he'd relinquished control over me when I was nine to a man who ended up hurting me very badly. Perhaps he believed that if he let me out of his sight this time, something worse would befall me. No doubt he was angry – with himself, with Poppa, perhaps even with Mum – for what had happened to me, but it came out as anger *against me*.

So instead of enjoying the freedom all school leavers long for, I became the only person at uni with a curfew, which got earlier every six months. If I arrived home after that curfew and a light was on in the house, I'd know Dad had waited up for me and that as soon as I walked in there would be hell to pay. I never did anything more racy than have the odd beer with my uni friends, but the moment I got home I faced Dad's scathing disapproval. He seemed to have no other way to express his concern for me. He believed that to stay safe I needed to change my behaviour and he thought that telling me I was losing my reputation was the only way to achieve this. But as far as I was concerned his fears were neither my fault nor my responsibility, and he should not have tried to make them so.

One major issue that developed was that Dad wouldn't accept any of my boyfriends, who all happened to be white Australians. Did he really never think back to when my grandmother was giving him such a hard time? Evidently not, and I didn't want to remind him for fear of his reaction. I don't think Dad's dislike of my boyfriends was ever about race, though. Like many fathers he no doubt thought that no young man would ever be good enough for me, whatever his colour.

Having said that, when I was still eighteen we all went back to India for a holiday, and I remember being terrified when I realised that one of my uncles was trying to set up an arranged marriage for me with one of my first cousins. Worse, Dad seemed to warm to the idea as our visit went on. Luckily, Mum stepped in smartly and called a halt to any such plan.

Perhaps another element of Dad's anger may have had something to do with his strict Muslim upbringing, where he had never been allowed to express his emotions. He also felt that his professional ambitions had been thwarted. When he saw me becoming a self-assured, confident young woman, he perhaps found it difficult to reconcile his ambitions for me with the reality of my independence from him. Like any other young person I wanted to make my own decisions about what to do with my life and to be allowed to make my own mistakes, in my own way. No doubt, Dad also wanted a say, but as far as I was concerned, it was my life now. I'd also become impatient with his insistence that being foreigners and Muslims meant we'd always be outsiders. And so, inevitably, we clashed.

The result of all this was that I found my early adult years bewildering and deeply troubling. At the time I found it extremely difficult to understand why Dad suddenly seemed to turn on me. I still felt protective towards him and I could appreciate my parents' many good qualities. But when Dad's insecurities and fears morphed into attacks on me and my morals, my empathy for him suffered.

I felt dismayed, disillusioned, sad, afraid – and heart-broken. The easy relationship we'd enjoyed disappeared when he started trying to control my every move. I'm still grieving for the end of that relationship and I'm still bewil-dered about what really happened. At the time I probably made it worse by simply getting on with my life, but I saw no other way. I refused to be the docile, compliant daughter he seemed to want.

I felt free going off to university each day but as soon as I arrived home again I felt trapped. As long as I was a poor, cash-strapped university student and had to live at home, I had to submit at least partially to Dad's will. But my love for tertiary education saw me through. I was growing intel-lectually. I tried to use what I was learning to reach out to my parents, particularly when I was studying psychol-ogy as part of my arts degree before eventually going on to law school.

At one stage I wrote a paper on child sexual abuse. I desperately wanted to talk to Mum and Dad about what had happened to me, and maybe even suggest family therapy to help heal old wounds. All I'd ever wanted to do since that whole ghastly period when I was nine was to try to make things right. But Dad would have none of it. 'If university is filling your head with ideas like this, then I'm pulling you out of university,' he said. It was a bit of an empty threat, said in anger, as I had a student loan and was working several jobs to support myself, so all he could really do was throw me out of his house. Luckily that was a threat he never acted on.

Dad had always known I wanted to study law, although when I eventually told him my areas of interest were criminal law and human rights law, he seemed bemused. For me it was a logical step. I felt I'd been denied justice as a child and so I wanted to help all those other people out there who felt as powerless as I had then.

I was trying to move out of home, but every time I made tentative attempts to find my own place, Dad would say that he and Mum would never talk to me again if I left, and that he'd die from a heart attack, like his own father. This wasn't a new tactic. For as long as I could remember, Dad had reminded us that everyone in his family died young – the implication being that he didn't have much time left either. It didn't help that he'd actually already suffered a heart attack. Whenever he wanted me to obey him, Dad would feign chest pains as a last resort. Now he used them to make me feel guilty about wanting to leave home.

Of course, now I wonder if his fear was actually the dread of losing something he loved: me. Everything he did – the things he said, his constant references to his supposedly fragile health – I see now as an attempt to keep me close to him. He just couldn't articulate it that way. Seen from the standpoint of my own generation, with its greater awareness of emotional intelligence, Dad – and Mum, for that matter – seemed hopelessly trapped within his inability simply to say

'I love you'. Instead, they both tried desperately to keep me with them.

My mother would almost always take my father's side, putting on a united front to try to make me feel guilty for upsetting, disappointing or angering them. When I commenced university Mum was a little more lenient with me than Dad was, but this caused tension between them, so she became stricter with me. She never openly took my side or challenged my father, or protected me from his anger.

My early memories of my mother are of a loving, affectionate woman who laughed a lot. She was quite a big, maternal figure of a woman, but always working. I spent a lot of time as a child on my own at home, at after-school or school holiday clubs, or looking after my young brother at home. I remember being taken to Mum's work when I was ill and hidden in the back tearoom while she would work a full day shift. I'm not sure whether it was out of financial necessity or whether her priorities were just very different to mine, but work seemed to come first in Mum's life and I remember always yearning for more time with my parents, which many of my school friends enjoyed with theirs.

I guess it was when I was in my mid-teens I started seeing my mother differently – perhaps as a flawed and complicated individual. It was at this point that my mother seemed quite subservient to my father, often relenting to his will and bearing the brunt of Dad's quick temper. Mum had started confiding in me when I was around fifteen or sixteen, telling me things that she was too afraid to tell Dad, mostly about financial issues and things that Dad's family in India had done and said that upset and annoyed her. Many of the things she would share with me were not really for the ears of a teenage daughter, but, although my parents had a lot of acquaintances that they called friends – they were always entertaining at home and going out to parties – I don't think Mum had any close friends she could confide in. So I had started to fill that role and felt, at that time, somewhat sorry for Mum, who appeared a little lonely and vulnerable and, at times, bullied by Dad.

Our relationship changed when I started university and the really intense difficulties with my father began. When my mother repeatedly refused to protect me or stand up for me, my resentment towards her grew.

Mum became a stronger, and, at times, more intimidating figure. She would do desperate and foolish things, particularly when it came to spending money, and she became quite cold and distant from me. It was like she was two different people: she could be overly friendly to others on many occasions but behind closed doors she was very judgemental and critical of them.

It makes me sad to think how different my relationship with my parents might have been had they been able to say what they *truly* felt. Instead, I spent those years feeling trapped and powerless.

In response to this dramatic change in my relationship with my family I felt a deep grief that seemed to pile on top of the grief I'd felt as a nine year old. What happened next seems now to have been inevitable, although at the time it was a desperate reaction. From my shock and horror that my parents weren't who I thought they were and my life wasn't what I thought it was – and certainly not what I'd thought it was going to be – emerged a feeling of utter despair. For a number of months darkness descended and I wanted to end my life *as it was*. That is to say, I didn't necessarily want to die; what I wanted was the life I was living to be over. But at that age – at that stage of my life – the two things seemed the same. It felt like the only way to make my parents understand what they were doing to me, to make them listen to me, to hear my cries and pleas, to give me a voice.

For a number of months, not long after my nineteenth birthday, I felt truly downtrodden and trapped. I turned to my mother for sympathy and support, only to be shunned by her.

I was starting to feel so depressed and desperate. At that time I truly felt that life would only get worse for me. I saw no way out of the controlling clutches of my parents and I desperately wanted them to know the damaging effect they were having on me. I felt like I was emotionally dying inside; I felt so abandoned and betrayed by my parents. So killing myself seemed like the only way I could make them see what they had done to me, and also the only way to end the suffering and turmoil I was in.

It got to the point that I drafted a suicide note in my head and made a plan: I would take an overdose of sleeping pills. Understandably, around this time I found it hard to concentrate on anything and my marks at university slipped. But I didn't tell anyone what I was going through – and no one asked, because I was becoming adept at putting on a brave face in public. By now I'd had lots of practice.

In the end my spirit and optimism for a better future shone through. I soon realised that taking my life was not the solution, and that my dreams of a better future and a career and life away from my parents were worth the continued pain and suffering. However, it was at about this time that I started seriously thinking about how I could leave home and escape their constant control and scrutiny.

I acknowledge, though, how desperate I was – and how desperate many other people feel at this vulnerable age. At the time it felt as though two rivers were converging: one was the life I'd believed I was living; the other was my life as it really was. Where those rivers met was a delta of lies and charades – I felt I could no longer trust my parents, that they'd been untruthful about who they were and how much care they were prepared to extend to me.

I see now that this darkness in my life had first appeared when I was nine, but at that age what could I have done with it? No child, no matter how mature, knows what to do with such a deep sense of despair. So I had to put it away. The first chance it had to resurface, however – when I was nineteen – it emerged with a vengeance. And it had company.

That I made it through that time without either taking my own life or indulging in behaviour that could have taken it for me seems like a small miracle. Except I know now that *I* got myself through that time. Increasingly, I began to look towards the future and think about what I could be. Escape seemed inevitable, and so my plans for independence began to take over.

I decided to go all out to achieve my dream of helping people who were powerless, and use my skills to achieve justice for those people. My parents supported my decision to study law and I was glad of this acceptance, but I lived in constant hope that they would accept everything else about me. I spent so many years trying to make things right. I begged my parents to go with me for counselling – I wanted to change them back to the people they'd been when I was in high school. Now I can see that I was probably fuelling the fire. After all, who the hell was I, their child, telling them they were doing things wrong and needed to become more enlightened?

What I really wanted was for them to be the best version of themselves – the version that had given my brother and me the gift of a wonderful education, of being tolerant of difference, of being broadminded and empathetic towards others. Those parents gave me a lot of gifts. Those were the parents I was trying to find once more.

I loved my parents. I love them still. When I reflect on this period of my life I can see that it taught me to survive hard knocks, to be resilient, and to do it with love and hope in my heart. I never gave up hope that my relationship with my parents could be restored. I never stopped believing that the bedrock of that relationship was our love for each other. We were a family. We still are.

What I learnt, though, was that only I could get myself through that time in my life. If I wanted help, then I had to help myself. And I'd have to learn the skills I needed on my own.

I've never regretted learning this lesson.

CHAPTER THREE

MY FIRST ANTHONY

Although my years at university were troubled with the disintegration of my relationship with my parents, there was one tremendous bright spot: Anthony. He was studying commerce at the same university. It didn't take long for us to become very serious about each other.

Just as my parents had faced fierce opposition from my maternal grandmother when they decided to get married, they in turn were completely against Anthony's plans to propose to me. By the time I was twenty-one – and Anthony twenty-three – we'd been in a relationship for more than two years and had started talking about a life together. Anthony arranged to hire a limousine, booked a helicopter ride over the city and reserved a table for us at one of the most exclusive restaurants in Perth for dinner one Saturday night, all of which he kept quiet from me. Anthony was like that: very thoughtful and a great romantic. Sometimes he'd collect me from university with a bunch of flowers in his hand and a gourmet picnic in the boot of the car. But all he said to me on this occasion was, 'Put on something nice. I'm going to take you out for a special evening.'

Before this evening took place Anthony went to see my parents to ask for their permission to marry me. Their reaction was immediate: they were furious. They told him there was no way this marriage would ever happen.

'Rabia and I love each other very much,' he said. 'I believe we're ready for marriage and I was hoping for your blessing – but I'm going to ask her anyway.'

My parents were horrified and, as I'd shortly find out, decided to try to put a stop to Anthony's proposal plans.

I had a Saturday job. Mum rang me at work and told me exactly what Anthony had organised for that night. She told me about the limousine, the helicopter and the restaurant – and she said that she and Dad would never speak to me again if I had dinner with Anthony and agreed to marry him. No doubt they thought we were both too young, and, knowing I was what they would have called 'headstrong', thought that threats were the only way to get through to me. They never gave any other reason, though, apart from our age. I suspected that they didn't want to give up control over me.

Distraught, I rang Anthony and told him about Mum's phone call. He was horrified and very upset, but we both felt we shouldn't let my parents stop us – even if the surprise was already spoilt. Anthony and I still had our special dinner, and he did propose to me, but what should have been an ecstatic, romantic, glorious surprise of a night was bittersweet. We were both very emotional, and I think that pushed us together even more. We decided that our love would win out regardless and that we would be together despite everything.

For the next few days my parents hardly spoke to me and wouldn't look at my engagement ring. Anthony was the first person to stand up to my parents on my behalf, so he became persona non grata in their eyes, at least for a short time. Knowing that I would marry Anthony whatever my parents' opinion but wanting their blessing nonetheless, I tried to play peacemaker. I begged them to talk to me and to share in my happiness. I said our marriage would happen no matter what and I wanted them to be a part of it. Anthony also came to the house and appealed to them.

In the end, they came around and seemed pleased about our engagement. It may have helped that Anthony's parents were very happy about it. As I said, I believe now that Mum and Dad thought the timing was wrong for Anthony and me to marry. They thought we were too young – and they were probably right. But part of the reason we wanted to get married when we did was that I was desperate to escape from my parents' house because they still wouldn't let me leave home. If I'd even suggested the idea of living with Anthony before we got married it would have probably killed my father – for real. So marriage was the only way out I could see. Having said that, I did truly love Anthony and genuinely wanted to be with him forever. It wasn't a cynical decision. I had plans for my life that weren't just about escaping my parents. I wanted to travel the world – and save the world. And I also wanted very much to be with Anthony.

During our two-year engagement, Dad ceased keeping such a close eye on my every move. I guess in my parents' minds, as I was about to become the wife of another man, there was no chance of me going off with 'a stranger', so there was no need for them to worry so much any more. They knew Anthony – and they knew I would be safe with him.

Anthony was a wonderful man and was very caring towards me. Unlike me, he was softly spoken and non-confrontational, and dealt with my parents by always treating them with respect and never challenging them. In other words, he went out of his way to make them like him – not cynically; it was just the way he was with people. And in the end they pretty much fell in love with him, too. He won them over the way my father had won over my grandmother: he killed them with kindness. He also got on well with my brother, and my brother adored him. So Anthony became family. He was the brother my own brother never had.

So calm was restored, and at the end of November 1994, at the age of twenty-three, I finished my law degree. A few days later, on 4 December, Anthony and I were married in the Uniting Church chapel at my alma mater, Penrhos College.

My parents had thrown themselves into the preparations for our wedding day, and it became a big public event. Half the wedding list was made up of their friends and business colleagues. I was so pleased they'd embraced our marriage to such an extent that they wanted their wider circle to celebrate it with them.

The moment Anthony and I were pronounced husband and wife was tremendous. I felt a huge sense of relief and liberation. Honestly, though, the house we'd bought together a couple of months earlier had become the real symbol of freedom for me. Anthony's parents, who were quite wealthy, had set up a trust fund for him, and one of its release triggers was his marriage. That, together with some of the money we'd saved, helped us buy a small tin-roofed Federation cottage in the affluent inner-city suburb of Subiaco. It had lovely wooden floors, a claw-foot free-standing bath and a huge back garden, which was the best thing going for it.

My parents were very involved in the wedding preparations. They contributed financially to the wedding, as did Anthony's parents, but in return they expected to invite many of their friends and my father's business associates. They loved public displays – no doubt bound up in the whole idea of 'saving face'. Anthony and I went along with their wishes, just to keep the peace, but I felt embarrassed because Anthony's parents were very down-to-earth people and a showy affair was not at all their style.

My father cried as I walked down the aisle. I knew they were tears of happiness as well as sadness. I was leaving home, all grown up. My mum was emotional, too. I could hardly believe that there I was, marrying the man I loved with my parents' blessing. So on that day I felt elation – and a little fear, too. For a minute or two during the wedding reception I became tentative about having married so young, although the elation returned when Anthony and I got into the wedding car to go to our hotel and I looked back at everyone and waved.

I knew that from this moment onwards, I'd never live with my parents again. I could determine the course of my own life. I'd make my own choices – and my own mistakes. I could finally start to discover who I was, beyond the tumult of so many difficult years. It was an exhilarating feeling.

It was freedom.

Chapter Four

BEGINNINGS AND ENDINGS

Anthony and I had a three-week honeymoon in Malaysia and the United States before returning to Perth. We set off again almost immediately after Christmas, bound for Singapore.

This wasn't part of our honeymoon. The accounting firm Anthony worked for had decided to send him to Singapore on a three-month posting, and luckily I was able to delay the start of my year doing articles – a requirement for legal practice – and go with him. So in the space of a month I'd gone from not being able to leave my parents' house without their permission to visiting three separate countries, one of them to live.

The accounting firm had organised a two-bedroom apartment in the middle of the city, which we shared with one of Anthony's colleagues who was there on a posting as well (albeit without his wife). Despite the constant heat and humidity, the city was buzzing – there were shops everywhere and people in them, visibly displaying their wealth. There was a large expat community full of young corporate types. Anthony and I lived an urban existence, away from the suburbs and poorer districts. I had no intention of becoming an idle expat, even for just three months, and within a couple of weeks I managed to get a short-term placement with Palakrishnan and Partners, a prominent Singaporean criminal defence firm. My work would offer my only insight into the 'real' people of Singapore and the social problems that beset this tightly controlled society. Ramanathan 'Pala' Krishnan, the managing partner, agreed to take me on for this period, basically as a favour to mutual family friends.

Earlier that year, Pala had been at the centre of a case that was reported around the world. He'd represented Michael Fay, an eighteen-year-old American who was caned for theft and vandalising cars, sparking debate in Singapore and inter-nationally about corporal punishment.

My own work at the law firm wasn't so high-profile. It was grim and it was sad. It involved helping to draft clemency applications for prisoners on death row at the city's notori-ous Changi Prison. Consequently, life in Singapore became interesting for reasons beyond the ordinary. I was occasionally followed by plain-clothes security men because of the sensi-tive nature of some of the cases I was working on. I spent a lot of time thinking about both corporal punishment and capital punishment. I never forgot how quickly, and with so little hesi-tation, a court could sentence an individual to death.

The work was sad and sobering because I'd interview the people who were trying desperately to keep hold of their lives. Many were drug traffickers who'd turned to such 'work' because they were desperate, vulnerable drug addicts themselves; or they were the mothers and fathers of drug addicts who'd tried to earn money by dealing in order to finance their child's habit or help them get treated. None of them were angels, but everyone had a story to tell that explained what had led them down this path.

As a young and idealistic lawyer, I did my best with their clemency applications but we were allocated barely twenty minutes to plead for each client's life one last time. It was like a sausage machine: dismissed, dismissed, refused, refused. Clemency applications were heard on a Wednesday. Friday was hanging day. Lives were extinguished with no further thought.

We knew that on Friday morning the fate of our client was sealed, which as a young barrister-in-training I found confronting and extremely depressing. I heard about only one case where a clemency application from a lawyer at Palakrishnan and Partners had succeeded, but in the time that I worked at the law firm not a single death sentence was overturned. This was not a reflection on the firm's lack of ability in these matters; it was just the way things were in Singapore.

Despite all the cases that ended in such harsh justice, in many respects I had a wonderful time in Singapore. Anthony's posting there provided us with an opportunity to live together far away from our families, which gave me a sense of freedom and control over my life for the very first time. I wished we could stay longer than three months.

When we returned to Perth, I started my articled clerkship. In 1995 Perth was still a small city compared with Sydney and Melbourne. Within legal circles everyone knew everyone else, so it was quite a cliquey place – but it was friendly nonetheless, with a sense of community. The physical beauty of Perth was as powerful as ever, and by this time the city was becoming more multicultural. There was, by this stage, lots of corporate money around as the era of the entrepreneurs – such as Alan Bond – had well and truly begun. My first job was at the Legal Aid Commission of Western Australia, as it was known in those days. There I quickly started specialising in criminal defence work. It was probably one of the best places for a young lawyer who wanted to become an advocate, because right from the start I was in court day in and day out. By my second year I was doing trials. Legal Aid was a brilliant training ground; as it was such a lean operation, its lawyers had to be able to do everything.

My stand-out experience was acting as junior counsel to the deputy director of Legal Aid in a High Court appeal that went on to become a landmark case. We had represented a man who was convicted for the murder of three people – his mother and two siblings – after a drug- and alcohol-fuelled rampage. He'd been sentenced to life without parole.

The High Court appeal we mounted was based on the principle of cruel and unusual punishment, since the convicted man was only seventeen or eighteen years old at the time he committed his crimes. We argued that to sentence someone so young to life in prison, with absolutely no prospect of rehabilitation or release, was cruel and unusual punishment and in breach of customary international law principles. We won the appeal, and that case further fed my appetite and passion for human rights work, which had been kindled during my years at university.

My passion for justice had never left me, and my desire for the truth always to be told was still my guiding star. As I had all my life, I wanted to give the silenced a voice and stand up for those who had no chance of standing up for themselves. Legal Aid work helped me do this because it was an opportunity to represent those who could not otherwise access or afford representation. I believed – and still do – that everyone deserved a voice in the justice system.

After about two years at Legal Aid, I moved to the Commonwealth Director of Public Prosecutions (DPP) and at the age of twenty-five became one of the youngest federal prosecutors in Australia at that time. I really was the baby of the office and I hoped like hell that I wouldn't disgrace myself. Those early years of practice truly were a baptism of fire, but I loved the work – not only was it varied but it was meaningful: I worked on drug importation prosecutions as well as prosecuting those whose greed had landed them in hot water.

Working at the DPP was always quite a challenge, not least because of the mental shift it required. I was reminded of this in particularly stark fashion when a defendant I would have represented once upon a time at Legal Aid threw a chair at me during my cross-examination. He was marched down to the cells for contempt of court and I was mercilessly teased by my colleagues when the story appeared in the papers the following morning.

I stayed in the DPP for a year without having any more chairs thrown at me, before deciding in late 1998 that the time had come to move to the United Kingdom to work. I had very grand dreams about what I wanted to do with my life, and I was determined it would involve seeking justice for others in the fields of both international criminal and human-itarian law. I was passionate about achieving this goal, which had become more important to me than anything else, but to achieve it I would have to leave Australia, where opportuni-ties to practise this sort of law were limited. I'd wanted to do this for at least three years but had pushed the desire to the back of my mind because, a couple of weeks after Anthony and I had returned from Singapore, I'd begun suffering from some very strange symptoms.

It was as if I had a really bad flu that wouldn't go away, and it was accompanied by chronic aches in my joints. Even more worryingly, I was passing blood. There followed a series of tests and medical appointments that lasted six months and led to an eventual diagnosis of lupus, an incurable autoimmune disease. (I don't suffer from it now, but am always mindful that it could return.) At that time not a lot was known about lupus, which can mimic other diseases. For a while they thought I had multiple sclerosis, then rheumatoid arthritis, and then chronic fatigue syndrome. At one point they were even enter-taining the thought of leukaemia. While I was relieved to finally have a diagnosis, I still didn't know much more than before; nor was there a lot of information available.

My ill health was a huge blow because it came just at the start of my career and my marriage. At times it was extremely difficult to work when I was ill, particularly when the disease was 'flaring', as it's called. In my worst periods of flare I could neither walk nor dress myself. Even having a shower was agony, because the water on my skin was so painful. It was dreadful. My poor husband had to do pretty much everything for me.

I also had to take high doses of steroids. When I was completely dosed up I felt like superwoman, but this was always followed by awful periods when I'd 'crash' and the disease would flare again. My body shape changed, too. Because of the steroids, I put on an awful lot of weight, and obviously that made me feel horrible. So for those two or three years it was tough.

Through it all, my desire to live and work in the UK remained, but I knew I had to be on top of the disease and free from steroids before I could achieve this. No one was sure why I developed lupus. My specialist had a theory that it was dormant in my system and had been activated by a type of virus together with some sort of emotional trauma. Personally, I believed it was the by-product of the emotional trauma I'd internalised for so long. The fact that it manifested just when I'd finally started to set up my own life seemed hugely unjust – yet strangely fitting. My mind was letting go, and so was my body.

This was pretty much the beginning of a pattern. Outwardly, no matter what was happening in my life, I was still able to get on with things, maintain a brave face and keep life ticking along. But invariably, despite my strong belief in mind over matter, my body would give out on me.

Lupus wasn't a great way to start married life, and any newly married couple would have found the going fairly tough, but my illness wasn't a factor in what happened next. Anthony was a wonderful man and an amazing husband, but by the time I was ready to leave for the UK we'd already drifted apart to the extent that we were simply good friends. It was almost as if we had gone through too much together. He'd seen the ugly, painful, dysfunctional side of my life close up, and was more or less acting as my parent rather than my husband.

I'd gone into this marriage making a commitment and I'd intended it to last all my life. I genuinely loved Anthony and felt safe with him, but the problem was that life was predictable. And I'd found out over the course of the marriage that predictability did not suit me.

There was also the fact that I wanted to move to the UK to make something of myself whereas Anthony was in a very different place. He was an extremely talented man with a commerce degree and a good job in an accounting firm, but he was content to keep along the path he'd chosen. There was absolutely nothing wrong with this, of course, but I realised that we'd become very different people. I guess I just had an extraordinary fire in my belly and a great wanderlust. Being content was simply not enough for me.

Anthony was such a good man, and perhaps the problem was my immaturity. I was young and idealistic and wanted to save the world – to go on big adventures, do charity work and use my knowledge as a lawyer to work with the dispossessed and those who had no voice. Anthony wanted a decent job, a house in a nice area, children and a dog. In other words, he wanted a happy domestic life, while travel, excitement, adventures and real freedom were the stuff of my dreams.

In my parents' eyes, Anthony could do no wrong and it was unreasonable of me to expect him to follow me to the other end of the world. In hindsight I find it strange that they didn't understand my need for travel, when they had spent their youth indulging their own wanderlust – my father as a pilot and then a purser, and my mother as a travel agent.

At the end of 1997, Anthony and I left for the UK together, even though we both knew our marriage was fracturing. One night earlier in the year we'd had a very sad conversation during which I explained that I just wasn't happy – and I'd given him no indication since then that the situation had changed. I think Anthony hoped our move to the UK would fix things. He was willing to indulge me by living overseas for a year or two, believing I'd get everything I wanted to do out of my system and that this would put our marriage back on track.

I already knew, though, that it would be the beginning of a whole new chapter for me. We can never know where life will take us, obviously, but I knew things would never be the same again. My world was expanding, and I could only dream about the possibilities that lay ahead.

CHAPTER FIVE

LONDON AND BEYOND

Anthony and I arrived in London and soon secured a double room at Goodenough College in Mecklenburgh Square, Bloomsbury, near Russell Square and Covent Garden in Central London, a well-known postgraduate residence for international students. The college was made up of three gorgeous Victorian buildings in a picturesque square with a large green in the middle, so it was a very pleasant place to live.

I found a job at one of the big 'magic circle' law firms, working as a solicitor doing public liability and commercial litigation work – a field of law that was completely out of my comfort zone. But it gave me a different sort of legal experience while I studied for my re-qualifying exams, which would eventually allow me to begin practising as a solicitor in England and Wales. (I was not in a position to join the English Bar, so I would work as a solicitor.) Plus the salary was good – which, in a city as expensive as London, was a consideration when taking the job. Anthony worked as an auditor for a large media outlet. Because we both earned fairly good money, we were able to pay the bills.

After getting over the initial culture shock of learning to live in such a busy, impersonal and fast-paced city, I quickly grew to love it, with all its history, its cosmopolitan lifestyle, opportunities and diversity.

To an outside observer it would have seemed as though we were on track – we had successfully moved halfway across the world, set up home and found work – but the cracks in our marriage only deepened after we arrived. The pressure of trying to adjust to a new life in the UK, along with finally being away from family tensions, dragged our relationship into the light. While it was clear to me that our marriage had run its course, though, there was a horrible period of about six months when Anthony, in denial about what was happening, understandably became quite angry and resentful. We were sharing the same bed, but awkwardly sleeping as far apart as we could in order to avoid physical contact.

We started having relationship counselling in 1999, but rather than helping us stay in the marriage, these counselling sessions made us realise it was time to part company. The sessions were healing and cathartic but also incredibly sad. And so, two years after our arrival in London, our marriage ended. Although this end was unpleasant, it was not acrimonious. We parted with mutual respect, genuinely wishing each other well. I still thought Anthony was a wonderful man, and we remained good pals. We just weren't meant to be married to each other, painful as that realisation was.

After Anthony moved out of Goodenough College to a flat with mutual friends, I moved into a single room and then psyched myself up to break the news to my parents. When I phoned them and told them the marriage was over, they were devastated. The whole family, including extended family and even my parents' friends, loved Anthony. We had been a very happy, very much in love couple for such a long time, and we had managed to keep up a brave front before leaving for London, so other people hadn't seen the collapse of our relationship. And being on the opposite side of the world made our splitting up even harder to understand for a lot of people – especially my parents.

Partly, my parents were embarrassed and humiliated to have a daughter who was a divorcée. They worried about what people would say. This may seem strange to many people, but saving face is hugely important in Asian culture – Dad's culture. Mum had taken on the values of his culture and so she, too, worried about saving face. The public self is the most important thing in some Asian families. It was certainly very important to mine, and never more so than when Anthony and I divorced.

My parents were also genuinely upset that Anthony was no longer a part of the family, and they were extremely concerned about my brother because Adam idolised Anthony. All of this broke my heart. I still wanted to please them; I'd never have upset them intentionally. But in spite of my best efforts it seemed I'd disappointed and upset them again. I felt alone in London. It was my own doing, certainly, but it was daunting all the same.

Although I knew that ending the marriage was the right thing to do, I decided I needed to get away from everything for a while. An unexpected opportunity presented itself within months. Goodenough College regularly invited guest speakers from all walks of life to give talks. I went along to one by a retired British Army officer, Colonel John Blashford-Snell, founder of the Royal Scientific Exploration Society.

The colonel had also been instrumental in starting up Raleigh International, one of Britain's best known international volunteer and expedition programs. He was looking for volunteers to join his community aid and scientific exploration trip to South America, otherwise known as the Kota Mama Expedition. The aim was to retrace the ancient Inca trade routes along the Amazon River while sailing in Inca-style replica reed boats, with volunteers stopping off at various places en route to take part in archaeological digs. At the same time, other members of the expedition would provide medical, dental and engineering support as well as other forms of aid work for local indigenous communities.

The colonel was looking for an assistant anthropologist and sponsorship officer to join the next expedition. I'd studied anthropology as a minor subject during my arts degree and had very much enjoyed it. So I decided to apply for the position and, much to my surprise, was accepted. My move in this direction wasn't as spontaneous as it might seem – call it catching up on lost time. For the first time in my life there was nothing to stop me from dropping everything to spend five months in South America. First, though, I enrolled in an intensive Spanish language course and took basic lessons in

70

Guarani, an indigenous Paraguayan Indian language. Then I took a leave of absence from my law firm, and I was off.

We had an extraordinary time on the Kota Mama Expedition. Together with the other volunteers, I took part in various community aid projects, carried out wildlife conservation tasks and met with tribal elders to discuss means of restoring law and order within their communities to reduce tensions between their tribes and their governments. I was part of a team that worked to build basic health clinics, schools and community halls for the local indigenous tribe. I would spend hours listening to their stories, learning what bound them as a group and also their history. Their optimism and happiness – despite having so little – really made an impression on me.

Some of the people on the expedition, really interesting people I came to admire, were members of the British Armed Forces. They were strong, as I'd expected army people to be; they could endure hardship and they had a lot of fuel in the tank for all sorts of things – again, as I'd mostly expected. But they were very charismatic people, which I hadn't expected; they had a sense of humour, they knew how to work hard, they knew how to play hard. I became friends with some of them and I realised we had a lot in common personality-wise – in fact, we were almost kindred spirits. So my preconceptions about what these people would be like – cliquey and stoic, not to mention killing machines – were completely blown away.

I developed a strong friendship with one of them in particular, a Royal Engineer and former bomb disposal

officer called Nathan Arnison. Arnie, as he was affection-
ately known, suggested I join the army as a legal officer. We
talked about this a few times while we were sailing down the
coast of South America, often as we watched a blood-red sun
set over the Amazon River. (Arnie later married one of my
closest friends, Laura, after a bit of successful matchmaking
on my part.)

During these journeys, Arnie talked about the opportunities for a military lawyer to work in The Hague and in
an international setting. He also pointed out that the job
demanded a vast amount of travel as well as adventure
training. All in all, he made life as an army lawyer sound
exhilarating and downright sexy. Everything he said about
travelling to different countries and working in human rights
law tallied with my long-held dreams about the direction my
life would take. But I needed time to think and catch my
breath; I'd just gone through a major change and I wasn't
quite ready for another one.

I returned to the UK at the end of the expedition feeling
refreshed and reinvigorated, but uncertain that the army was
where I should be heading. I resumed my job at the same law
firm as before, but by now I'd requalified as a UK solicitor
and knew the commercial side of law wasn't for me. Initially
I decided to go back to criminal law, where I'd started, and
I plotted a course I hoped would help me make a name
for myself as a criminal defence solicitor in England. This,
I hoped, I could use as a springboard into something on a
grander scale that would allow me to do more to help people.
All I ever wanted was to use my skills and learning to help

people – to give them a voice and access to justice. I wanted to do this on as large a scale as possible, where I could make the most difference.

I moved out of Goodenough College to share a house with two other girls, Kate and Justine, in Camberwell, South London, a move made possible by another of my new friends from the expedition, a man called Charles Sturge, who'd been the expedition photographer and has since made a name for himself as a commercial photographer. Life in Camberwell couldn't have been more different from that in the college. For nine months I lived in a three-bedroom Victorian terrace in an eclectic, working-class, predominantly black part of London. There was a working-man's pub at one end of our road and an Asian corner store at the other. Although things had changed in so many ways, I had lots of laughs with the girls and seemed to have found myself in just the right place at the right time.

About six months after I moved, I started looking for a position as a criminal defence lawyer. I managed to find one at a reasonably good level that would see me pretty much running a criminal law practice in Leeds, in the north of England. This seemed the perfect first step on the career path I'd mapped out, so I packed up, moved to Leeds and rented a place – a two-up, two-down stone terrace country cottage – in a pretty, quiet North Yorkshire village set in the middle of fields. There was one shop and one petrol station.

I worked in Leeds for the next nine months or so, but I became very lonely during that time. A lot of my friends were in London or near it. The job was good, but I needed more than that to enjoy my life, and however much the money was it could never replace good friends. I loved the Yorkshire people, who were so down-to-earth and friendly, but found the area too cold and wet, despite the rolling hills and hip nightlife.

So I applied for another position, in Somerset this time, running a criminal practice for a Bristol firm. Working as a criminal defence lawyer in county England wasn't in the slightest bit dull. No two days were the same, and while work was busy and clients were plentiful, life in my stone house in a very pretty village between Bristol and Bath – the first home I'd bought all on my own – was peaceful, comfortable and utterly liberating. My home was in a quiet cul-de-sac and had a view of the Somerset hills.

I enjoyed living in such a beautiful, historic part of England, with its rolling green fields, canals and gorgeous historic stone buildings. Bristol was a smaller, funky version of London and offered great cafés and nightlife, as well as allowing me to build a name for myself as a criminal lawyer Bristol was also home to two other friends I had met on the South America expedition, John Teague and Ilia Hayes.

I was completely in control of my destiny – and making all my decisions on my own. This was something I'd wanted for so long, and was so different from what I was used to. Moreover, the most remarkable thing about me now seemed to be not my 'foreign' background or my blue-eyed, olive-skinned appearance, but the fact that I had an Australian accent. My name also occasionally attracted a bit of atten-tion, but not in a negative way. It was refreshing to be almost anonymous after a childhood spent being 'different'.

But while life in Somerset was very pleasant, Arnie's suggestion that I join the British Army remained at the back of my mind. So just for the heck of it, in March 2001 I took a big step and submitted an application for a commission with the British Army Legal Services (ALS). I believed the army would provide me with the opportunity to work in the field of international humanitarian law and, given the resources of the army, help people on a larger scale than I would have been able to elsewhere. So the army was a means to an end – or, really, a higher goal.

About seven weeks later, the army wrote and asked me to report to a selection panel in Hampshire. Arnie had given me a good idea of the basic tests I'd have to pass to be selected for the army. So while I continued working full-time as a criminal defence lawyer, I trained once or twice a day, every day, trying to improve my fitness by running and swimming, and my strength by doing weights and push-ups. The selection process for the army was run over a few days in May 2001. It was challenging and mostly consisted of several rounds of interviews, psychometric tests and physical command and leadership tests.

My employers at the Bristol law firm, who knew I was considering a career in the military, tried to tempt me to stay on by offering promotion and partnership prospects. Financially, this should have been the more attractive and preferred option, but by this stage I was becoming excited and seduced by the possibility of life as a military lawyer.

I had a great group of friends in Bristol, and friends from London also visited me regularly. They were mostly very supportive of my decision to join the army, although some thought I was crackers and made lots of jokes about *G.I. Jane* and *JAG*. Even at this point, though, I didn't start seriously weighing up my choices or doing a lot of thinking about a future in the military, as I really didn't think I stood much of a chance of being selected.

That moment came about seven weeks later, when the ALS recruiting colonel phoned to offer me a commission. I was at the County Court in Bristol when the call came through, and remember taking off my wig and standing in front of the mirror in the barristers' robing room, studying my reflection, trying to make this huge decision about what to do. I think the recruiting colonel was taken aback when I didn't say yes straight away and instead told him I needed time to think about it.

He replied, 'Don't take too long because we have a long list of people who would jump at the chance.'

I thought back to my conversations with Arnie in South America. I remembered him saying the army would be a great opportunity to do something different and to experience exciting adventures. But it was still such a strange idea – the army is not presented as a possible career path for graduating lawyers. When I'd finished my degree I'd had no idea it was even possible. It was only by talking to Arnie that I knew lawyers for the British Army worked at The Hague and other international posts, that they conducted courts martial and worked in international humanitarian law. This was the work I had dreamt of doing: prosecuting war criminals, protecting and seeking justice for the victims of war, inhumanity and genocide. I also enjoyed being a court advocate, so courts martial appealed to my sense of justice, as they ensured that soldiers who broke the rules and committed crimes were rooted out.

In the end, it was the memory of those conversations with Arnie that swayed me. Joining the army, I decided, was exactly what I needed to do now. I was ready.

So I rang the recruiting colonel back and accepted the offer. A few months later, in September 2001, I was formerly commissioned as a captain in the British ALS. Just before taking up my commission and starting the officer training course, I took a couple of weeks off and went to Greece for a quick break with a girlfriend from my Goodenough College days. My plan was then to fly back to London and, that same day, take another flight directly to Australia. This was pushing it, but I knew it might be the only opportunity I'd get for a while to see family and friends. I planned to stay in Perth for about ten days, which would give me plenty of time to explain to my family why I was joining the army – because I knew they would have a lot of questions.

I'd already explained to my friends in England that I felt the army would provide me with the structure to do the sort of work I'd dreamt of, and on a much larger scale. Their support was important to me. None of my British friends were worried about me as a Muslim joining the army, because none of them really identified me with Islam. Nor did my Australian friends, if it came to that. My Muslim background was never the sort of thing that featured in our lives or conversations, and I'd never made a big deal about it.

The most my friends seemed to register was that I had an Arabic name and didn't eat pork.

Naturally, I wondered what my parents would say about my decision to join the army once I got back to Perth, even though I'd already forewarned them that I was applying. This was uppermost in my mind when I organised my flights from Greece back to London, and then on to Perth. The tickets were booked for what should have been just another day on the calendar: Tuesday, 11 September 2001.

CHAPTER SIX

AFTER SEPTEMBER 11

Our bus was still about thirty-five minutes away from Heathrow when the driver suddenly turned up the volume on the radio. For everyone who heard that report – or was already watching the horrors unfolding on TV – life came to a standstill.

The BBC was reporting news of unprecedented terrorist attacks in New York. The World Trade Center's South Tower had just collapsed. A second plane had flown into the North Tower, which had been hit first but at this stage was still burning. On the bus, there was stunned silence. By the time we reached Heathrow and made a dash for the TV monitors inside the terminal, both towers were gone. Everywhere I looked, people seemed dazed. I don't think anyone was able to absorb fully what had just happened in the US. The Twin Towers had been 110 storeys high and an instantly recognisable part of New York's skyline. I'd visited them myself, not long before.

Even at this early stage, Osama bin Laden's name was already all over the news bulletins, and at every checkpoint in Heathrow, men and women dressed in traditional Arab and Muslim dress were being given a very hard time by the airport's security staff. I was wearing Western clothes as usual, but when I handed over my passport, for a few, startling moments I felt as if I was being scrutinised. Perhaps I was being overly sensitive and just imagining it, although it's highly likely that anyone with a Muslim or Arabic name would have attracted extra attention that day. I didn't feel angry or resentful. To be honest, I was far more preoccupied with another thought: that the attacks in the US would change the face of modern warfare for the foreseeable future. And that future had just become mine.

Immediately after the September 11 attacks, assumptions were made about all Muslims, regardless of their background. Suspicion, rage and fear abounded, and it became extremely important that those who understood Islam – as opposed to the radicals who had committed the attacks and their ilk – brought some sense of balance and perspective and worked within the systems and institutions of affected countries, hopefully to temper any action and response. The armed forces of the UK and the US, and those who worked within their governments, needed to be educated about the truth: that being Muslim didn't mean that someone was automatically a radical out to destroy non-Muslim societies.

The tension at Heathrow Airport because of the tough security checks seemed to follow us onto the plane back to Perth. The flight took fourteen hours longer than usual because our route had been changed so that we flew around the Middle East, effectively avoiding it. There was a complete news blackout on board – even the radio stations were switched off – so we had no way of knowing whether more planes had been flown into buildings in the US, or anywhere else. There was hardly any talking among the passengers. I'll never forget the quietness, the almost complete absence of conversation.

My parents were at Perth Airport to greet me. They were as shocked as everyone at the news and were quite emotional when they saw me. Given how late my flight was, their imaginations had run riot, so they were glad to see me safe. And I was relieved to have arrived safely, but desperate for news of the attacks. Once I had an opportunity to talk to them about my decision to join the army, I learnt it wasn't something they'd expected at all, in spite of my father's own early military ambitions and the fact that I had already forewarned them of my decision. They had so many questions, and I knew they had doubts about my decision and whether or not I had really thought it through. The army was not something they had ever planned for me – in fact, they thought I was mad to do it, especially then, with the aftershocks of the September 11 attacks reverberating around the world. Dad was particularly worried about the decision I'd made. But I don't think they realised how big my dreams were.

I don't think my parents, or many other people in Australia, though, fully appreciated the gravity of what had happened and what might follow as a result, even though there was a lot of talk about al-Qaeda and the likelihood of its involvement in the attacks. In truth, I think what most concerned my father was how I'd be viewed as a foreigner, and as a Muslim, in the British Army – an army he'd only encountered as a small child as part of British rule in India.

When he asked me within hours of my return how I thought British soldiers would react to a Muslim woman joining their ranks, my response echoed what I'd always said in the past: 'Being Muslim doesn't define me. I get on well with people – and people don't immediately identify me with Islam. When they do, fine, but I'm not just about that.' I also explained that I was determined to be an army lawyer and pointed out that I'd be using all my skills to do good for others.

I suspect, though, that my parents thought joining the army was the equivalent of an early – a *very* early – midlife crisis for me. If the dynamics of our relationship had been different, I might have interpreted what they said as an extension of their usual concern for my happiness and well-being, and it probably was. But at the time I thought they were just worried about what people would think of me.

My parents' negative reaction made my trip home sadder. I wanted them to be part of my life, to share in my happiness at reaching what I felt was an important decision and the opportunity for a wonderful new career path. But it wasn't to be. So after a very rushed and emotional trip, I returned to the country that had started to feel more like my home.

Once I was back in the UK, I reported for duty at ALS Headquarters before setting off to start the professionally qualified officers course at Sandhurst, the Royal Military

Academy in Surrey. My fellow 'students' included other lawyers, as well as doctors, nurses, dentists, vets and chaplains. By this stage, because of the September 11 terrorist attacks, the army had suddenly become a very different military from the one I'd planned to join. Now the prospect of some kind of activity in the Middle East loomed large. But I had no second thoughts.

Our course was an abbreviated version of the year-long course undertaken by regular officers, but it was still extremely physically challenging. We had to pass all the major skills tests like any other officer: weaponry, physical agility and endurance, signals basics, marching drill, day and night exercises. We also had command tasks, such as getting a case of rifles up a hill and over a stream using just our bare hands and rudimentary tools. I broke my nose during one of these training exercises, and also severed my finger. There were all sorts of trials and tribulations, and completing the course was a significant achievement for me. Not just that: I found that army life really suited me. The structured, ordered and organised way of life appealed to me, as did the freedom to spend downtime participating in team sports and adventure training. (I received scuba diving qualifications while in the army.) Food, cleaning and accommodation were all taken care of, and I found myself among like-minded people – positive, strong personalities who were driven and motivated, as I was.

At university my political views had been fairly left-wing; I'd very much believed in freedom and people's rights. I'd even started my career at Legal Aid, which was traditionally where left-leaning law students went. Given that, the army was the last place I should have ended up, and I should have hated it for all it represented. Instead, I took to it like a duck to water. I think I saw it all as one big challenge.

The regimentation of army life – including the giving of orders – was not that much different to what I had grown up with. I even found that I enjoyed learning skills such as shooting – but I never contemplated the possibility of taking a human life, as combat soldiers had to do. As a lawyer, it was unlikely that I would ever have to fire a shot. My mind and my words were my weapons.

At Sandhurst they tried to 'break' us and then build us up again, in order to find out who was the 'real deal' and whether or not we could cope with the sorts of situations we'd encounter in the army. There was a lot of physical, mental and emotional testing. I approached all of this with a bit of humour – because I didn't take them or myself too seriously – but I still played the game. Another part of me just saw it as a challenge – I was determined not to let them break me. Officer training at Sandhurst was the first time I realised that I thrived on that sort of pressure and adrenaline, as well as the structure and the discipline. It was all a bit of a revelation for me. Given how I had also thrived at Penrhos College, my high school, I began to realise that I liked the sense of belonging and identity a uniform brought. I guess that makes me a conformist, but I believe that it was the sense of belonging to a group – and a fairly rarefied one at that – which was the attraction. The rules of army life in and of themselves were no attraction – I just put up with them, as they didn't really cause me any hardship.

I was delighted when my parents agreed to fly over for my passing-out parade, but they could only stay for forty-eight hours and, because of my training commitments, I was hardly able to spend any time with them. Nevertheless, the passing-out parade was a proud moment for them. They also got to meet some of my friends, who came out in droves to support me. When Mum and Dad said goodbye after their lightning visit, I was very emotional. It meant so much to me that they'd come to see me achieve something so big.

I was unable to see them off at the airport. Straight after the passing-out parade, I had to pack up and leave Sandhurst to travel down to ALS Headquarters in Wiltshire, where I was due to start my six weeks of specialist military legal training. Those days of their visit, the passing-out parade and the move to Wiltshire were like a whirlwind that tossed me from my old life into my new one. It was confusing and exciting all at the same time.

Once I arrived in Wiltshire, it became clear that we'd been existing in a little bubble at Sandhurst. We'd been in an extremely intense environment where they'd tried to fill us with as much knowledge as possible. Now we concentrated on the areas of law we would be practising as military lawyers, which included international humanitarian law and military discipline law.

From memory, there was very little, if any, discussion or reference to the terrorist attacks in the US during any of my training. It was very much business as usual. I think the training staff made a conscious decision not to allow September 11 to distract them or us from the job at hand.

But, of course, the attacks and aftermath were always in the background. We were hearing information about operations and deployments that were being planned by the Americans, and people kept asking when the Brits were going to get involved. The British Army was initially deployed to Afghanistan in October 2001, but that didn't affect us significantly in terms of the ALS, since British involvement at that stage was more or less restricted to Special Forces. So our training continued as planned.

My thirtieth birthday was coming up, and after a spectacular combined birthday party with my friend Laura, I was posted off to Northern Ireland for three months with the Royal Scots, the oldest infantry regiment in Britain. This was when I started learning what it was like to be a soldier, and it was a very steep learning curve indeed. An attachment with the infantry was all part of the training regime. You were expected to live and work full-time with the members of the regiment for three months, in order to learn soldiering skills and to find out what life was really like as an army soldier and officer.

Our job in Northern Ireland was to maintain a stable environment. Despite the Troubles being all but over, there was still some loyalist activity in the form of roadside bombs. Northern Ireland police officers were still being murdered, as were British Army personnel. The situation remained tense. So during those three months I was very focused on what was going on, and making sure that I didn't let my fellow soldiers down. The tour was an opportunity for me to embed myself among soldiers and learn the pressures, realities and challenges the soldiers faced. I assisted with some headquarters research work, took shifts as a watchkeeper (monitoring calls and operation reports in the Ops Room), participated in public order and riot control training and often went out on patrol with the troops, where I soon got used to being abused and spat at by Ulster youths.

At the end of my three months, I came back to England tougher, fitter and even more committed to a career in the military.

My first posting, in March 2002, was to the Army Prosecuting Authority (APA), which was based in Uxbridge, in Greater London. There I carried out the role of a prosecutor, but of military offences in a military court. We were kept fairly separate from the rest of the army, as our job was often difficult and unpopular, as we were prosecuting other members of the armed forces.

Posting me there was an easy decision for the army to make because I'd previously worked as a prosecutor and I was a criminal law specialist. I spent the next two years prosecuting some quite high-profile courts martial in England, Scotland, Northern Ireland and Germany – at one time coordinating the prosecution of the largest ever army fraud ring, which involved more than twenty separate trials, most based in Northern Ireland. I also prosecuted soldiers for violent offences, sexual offences, and for dishonesty, and advised the Royal Military Police on a number of high-profile criminal investigations.

During this time I came to discover more about myself while seeing more of the world. I'd always felt that I was strong – strong-minded and strong-willed, but also strong in my ability to bear a lot of what life had to throw at me – but I think the army honed that. It gave me a disciplined and focused way to draw upon my strengths and taught me how to lead people. Some of the necessary qualities I had naturally, such as how to relate to people from all walks of life, from all parts of the world, and not to be intimidated by rank. I was able to communicate with all sorts of people from all socioeconomic backgrounds as well, from the private soldier from a rough background right up to the senior, senior commanders who should otherwise have intimidated me.

That ability to relate to all sorts of people came, no doubt, from my childhood – specifically from the time when my parents and I moved from India to Australia. I was out of place in the country that became my home, so in order to find my place I had to learn to relate to the people I found there. I believe I learnt empathy at that young age, and once I was in the army that translated into a desire to use my skills, experience and talents – everything I'd learnt – to give a voice to others who weren't so well equipped or well resourced.

When I wasn't living out of a suitcase as a travelling prosecutor, I played a lot of hockey and soccer on military teams. I also became involved in a masochistic exercise class called the 'Hour of Power' and trained for the London marathon. The latter started off as a dare, but then I agreed to run the marathon for charity.

Training for the marathon was hard, but when I set my mind and commit to something I *always* see it through. I enjoyed finally overcoming my loathing of running. I loved pushing my body to its limit and surprising myself as to what

I was capable of. I'm also a bit of an adrenaline junkie! On the day itself I had a respectable run. As soon as I crossed the line my first thought was that I had to do it again – and raise more money and manage a better time.

At about this time, I realised it was unlikely I'd ever return to my house in Bath, which I'd rented out, so I sold the house and started living in the Officers' Mess in Uxbridge. Here just about everything was taken care of – including, oh bliss, cleaning and cooking.

By the time I joined the APA, everyone in the armed forces knew the Cold War days were well and truly over. The period when the British Army was spread between the UK, Germany and Northern Ireland was over as well. The most recent operations involving the British military had been the Falkland Islands, Gulf War One and the Balkans War. An era had ended. It was obvious the armed forces were about to enter a volatile new stage.

Now all the talk was about Afghanistan, the American reaction to the September 11 attacks and to al-Qaeda, the rooting-out of terrorists, and the dreaded 'war on terror'. We knew that wherever the Americans went, we would eventually follow, since that was clearly the relationship the British Government was fostering with the US administration. Then, in March 2003, when I was still only halfway through my posting with the APA, Britain joined the US, Australia and Poland in the invasion of Iraq.

As I was approaching the end of my posting, in February 2004, the talk among my colleagues was that it was only a matter of time before we'd be facing a prosecution under war crimes legislation as a result of the war on terror. Accordingly, preparations were being made for these possible future courts martial. Initially I thought the preparations for these prosecutions would be what exercised my colleagues and me. A lot of work was being done on the United Nations resolutions and interpretations of international laws and conventions regarding what was legally possible. There was also the drafting of memoranda of understanding and status of forces agreements that would eventually need to be put in place when Saddam Hussein's regime was overthrown and a temporary Iraqi Government was appointed by the Coalition.

In short, all kinds of legal underpinnings had to be dealt with before such a deployment could go ahead. Most of the work that was being done, however, involved justifying the invasion. Not much thought or work was going into the aftermath – in other words, the plan that was to be followed once Saddam had been ousted.

I knew a lot of my superiors in the ALS were involved in the work I've just mentioned, but I thought I was too junior to be a part of it. The first real British military response to September 11, in which military lawyers like me became part of the action, took place during the months leading up to the invasion, when we attended a lot of meetings and seminars held by the ALS that dealt with the legal justification for the Iraq campaign.

I might have been relatively junior as an army lawyer, but I was an experienced legal practitioner, and I remember being uncomfortable with the alleged justification under international law concerning Britain's involvement in the initial invasion period. From a legal point of view, it didn't sit well with me in the beginning – and I wasn't the only one. Quite a few of my colleagues shared my misgivings, and I remember having discussions with them about it. So there was some disquiet in the legal corps, although of course some officers were dying to see action – the 'bring it on' brigade, as I called them. But although I began to start feeling a little concerned about my decision to join the army, I knew I'd follow my orders whenever they were handed down.

I understood, as we all did, that the then British attorney-general, Sir Peter Goldsmith, had said that UK participation in the Iraq invasion was lawful, based on his interpretation of the UN resolutions. (Although the nature of his advice would become controversial later on, because he'd previously provided contradictory advice to the prime minister, Tony Blair.) This made me feel a little better, since it was advice from the very top echelons of government, and therefore the decision was out of the armed forces' hands. It was an executive decision that we were going in.

I became less concerned about my role in the army and in the institution, therefore, but I was still concerned as an international lawyer. And as we know now, the international legal community eventually recognised that there was insufficient, or at least questionable, justification in international law for the initial invasion. We also know now that Tony Blair's own cabinet ministers warned him against the Iraq campaign.

If I had other qualms, they were to do with a powerful premonition I'd had a few days after September 11. I'd suddenly sensed strongly that I had to continue down the path I was now on, as a newly joined-up member of the British Armed Forces. I felt, on a very deep level, that my Muslim background, in combination with my legal skills, would have major consequences in the future. We all have premonitions – instinct or intuition, if you prefer those terms – but we tend to dismiss them. For all my upbringing in a 'rational' household, I'd always believed in the power of intuition. And I believed in karma and destiny: the notion that certain things in our lives are already written and must come to pass. So perhaps the feeling I had in the wake of September 11 was my fate catching up. But it hadn't stopped the 'rational' part of my brain wondering whether the fact that Islam as a religion and Muslims would be under constant suspicion from then on might affect or challenge me personally, as well as in my job.

There was something else, too: I knew there would be instances where I'd have to give unpopular advice during a very stressful or time-critical situation, to high levels of military command – and I wondered how I'd deal with that. Because I was in my early thirties by this time – and more self-assured about my legal abilities – the latter situation didn't trouble me so much. I was certain that if a situation ever arose where I had to advise strongly against something, such as calling off a military strike, I'd do my utmost to give that advice, even though the operational decision would ultimately be down to the commander. As long as I did my job and documented it, I'd know I'd done all I could and fulfilled my duties as a military lawyer.

The one thing I didn't predict was that I'd be posted to Iraq so soon after joining the army, even though I had wondered whether my new employer would take advantage of my background and use me sooner rather than later because of that, or keep me away from the battlefields *because* of my background. I'd hoped they would use me.

In the meantime, I started learning a bit more about Islam. I was becoming increasingly frustrated by the ignorant view constantly expressed in public that all Muslims were radical, that acts of terrorism were acts of Muslims, and that Islam was undemocratic. It was clear to me that Islam was being marginalised and demonised.

I regard myself as Muslim by birth and so I see Islam as part of my cultural and ethnic identity rather than a formal religion that I practise. I appreciate some of the Islamic customs (for example the belief that we leave this world the same way we come into it and so when we die we are buried in a single white cloth in a simple ceremony), am aware of the teachings of Islam (in particular the Five Pillars) and struck by the similarities between Islam, Christianity and Judaism.

I have a respect for the religion and its teachings, although, apart from not eating pork, I do not formally or outwardly practise Islam. I do, however, identify even more strongly with my Indian heritage. I cook and eat traditional, authentic Indian cuisine, share many of the ideals and values of Indian people (spirituality, importance of food as a way of showing love and friendship, respect for elders, importance of sharing wealth by giving back to the community and the needy). But I am not blind to what I perceive as some of the faults or weaknesses of both the practise of Islam and Indian culture.

I find the way that some Muslim communities practise the religion challenging, particularly the orthodox Muslims and their sexist attitude towards women and girls. I also believe that so many problems have arisen from the caste system in India. The gap between the haves and the have-nots widens all the time and the lack of empathy and humility that I have seen many young, wealthy, educated Indian people display is disappointing and worrying. No one should be treated like a second-class citizen just because they are of a lower caste or have less wealth. With regards to Islam I am more comfortable with the liberal practice of the religion, particularly those communities that encourage and support women to be educated and free thinking. All of my impressions of Islam as practised in the Middle East were, of course, viewed from my perspective in the UK. I'd never been to Iraq; nor had I ever had plans to visit. Now I was going, everything I thought I knew – about law, about Islam, about the army and about myself – would be tested. There was no way around that. This was what I'd signed on for when I joined the army, even if it wasn't exactly what I'd imagined. But what I'd wanted to do, always, was act to ensure that human rights were protected – and where would that be needed more than in a theatre of war?

CHAPTER SEVEN

THE SECOND, COMING OF ANTHONY

During my posting to the APA, I met the man who would become my second husband. He was an officer in the Royal Air Force and his name, believe it or not, was Anthony. We were on the same RAF base in Uxbridge, near London, where Anthony was an air traffic controller. He was my neighbour in the Officers' Mess, and we were friends for about a year before we started dating, in January 2003.

We knew very early on that we wanted to be with each other forever. The connection was immediate. He proposed to me within three months, and we became engaged in April that year. I had a number of phone conversations about Anthony with my parents, who seemed happy for me, but I knew they would want to meet the new man in my life.

So in the Christmas of 2003, a few months after my father had triple bypass surgery and Anthony had returned from a short deployment to Iraq, I took Anthony to Perth to meet my family for the first time. He'd never been to Australia before and was looking forward to the trip. To prepare him for meeting my family, I told him, 'I am who I am because of my parents, and in spite of my parents.' It was how I felt.

The first week back in Perth, when we were living at my parents' house, was very pleasant. Anthony, Mum and Dad got along extremely well. Then we all went off to spend our usual week on the south-west coast in a big house my parents had rented for the occasion. My brother, his girlfriend and her parents joined us, as usual, along with some close friends of Anthony's and mine from the UK. The party also included some old family friends, so it was a big group.

I'd brought along some samples of Indian materials and styles of wedding invitations to show my parents, and explained to Mum and Dad that I wanted to honour my Indian culture as part of the wedding. I was trying to involve them and make them happy, but they didn't seem as pleased or interested as I'd expected.

My brother, who is keen on food and wine, chose the itinerary each day, which meant he, his girlfriend and her parents, together with Mum and Dad and their friends, spent a lot of time at wineries or having expensive lunches. Anthony and I and our UK friends never seemed to be invited on these daytrips, which I found quite embarrassing, so I organised separate outings for us.

I was completely blown away at the end of the week when my parents gave me an absolute mouthful. It turned out they were furious that we'd gone off and done our own thing. In vain, I tried to point out that I'd arranged to take Anthony and our friends sightseeing because we hadn't been invited on any of the daytrips organised by my brother. Perhaps they had just thought we would know we were invited and were offended when we never turned up where they were going. But how could we have known we were invited if they never said?

They didn't say now. Instead they blamed everything on Anthony. 'He's changed you,' they said. 'He's trouble. We don't like him, we don't accept him and we think you're making the biggest mistake in the world.' I think what they meant by this was that I was no longer falling into line and following the family's wishes like a sheep. I was not passive, compromising and resigned. But why would I have been? I now had someone in my life I wanted to show off my home to – someone whose wishes I was concerned about above all others', and someone I wanted to make happy. I wanted Anthony to have a great holiday. I wanted my friends to enjoy themselves too. And I believe that having Anthony and my friends there gave me the confidence to make decisions for myself. My parents didn't like this – they wanted to make decisions for me. But that was never going to happen again.

I'd hoped for something wonderful when I brought Anthony home to meet my parents. I'd expected them to make us both feel special and important (as they had done at the beginning of our stay), and thought they would want to spend lots of time with us. Instead, they said they wouldn't speak to me again if I married him.

I was shocked. Part of their response, I was sure, was wrapped up in the fact they'd been so fond of my first husband and wished he was still part of the family.

But perhaps they also felt that my relationship with Anthony meant I would be forever beyond their reach. In their own way, they probably wanted a reconciliation as much as I did, but in their view the presence of Anthony made this impossible. Their opinion would never matter to me as much as his would. They would never again be able to influence my decisions and my actions. They could never be my all again.

Anthony developed a very strong dislike for my parents from this point.

I cut the holiday short. We were supposed to spend three or four weeks with my parents, but I couldn't allow Anthony to live under their roof when they'd made it clear they wanted nothing to do with him. We quickly arranged a trip over to Adelaide to see my family there. I was particularly close to my mother's brother, Uncle Kevin, and wanted to see him. In Adelaide, we tried as best as we could to rescue the holiday. My uncle, in contrast to his sister, became very fond of Anthony very quickly.

After Adelaide we went on to Sydney, where we met up again with our UK friends and spent a few happy days together before returning to Perth for just one day to take the return flight to London that evening. My parents knew we would be back in Perth, and that we would be there for a whole day. I'd convinced myself they would try to get in touch and smooth things over, but I didn't hear from them.

It was a very hot day, and by the time we boarded our flight I was in a bad state. My face was puffed up and my eyes were stinging with crying. Despite being with Anthony, I felt disappointed, abandoned and heartbroken. I'd never really given up on the idea of restoring my relationship with my parents and brother to the point before everything had gone awry. I was still the little girl who adored her baby brother and loved her parents more than anything. That was who I wanted to be always. For years, I'd clung to this idea without even realising I was clinging. Any show of affection from my parents – like coming to Sandhurst – made me believe anew that we could get back to the way we used to be.

Now, at a point when everything in my life seemed to be falling into place – I was doing work that had meaning for me and I'd found my great love in Anthony – I'd expected my family to be happy for me. But whenever we seemed to reach common ground, it disappeared beneath our feet. But this time Anthony had seen it all. It wasn't in my head. I wasn't making it up. The disintegration of my relationship with my family was *real* – and that meant it was probably permanent, too.

As we flew out of my home town, I began crying again. Already I knew it would be a very long time before I could bring myself to return. It does, after all, take a long time to recover from a broken heart.

CHAPTER EIGHT

ORANGES AND LEMONS . . .
AND THEN OFF TO IRAQ

Anthony and I married in London in July 2004, at St Clement Danes on Strand in London. It's the Central Church of the RAF, and most famous for its appearance in the childhood song 'Oranges and Lemons, Say the Bells of St Clements'.

In the weeks leading up to the wedding, close friends of mine, as well as Uncle Kevin and Anthony's mum, Kath, made several attempts to talk my parents into changing their minds about the marriage. They all told Mum and Dad how much I wanted their blessing, what a big mistake they were making about Anthony, and how they would regret their decision not to be at my wedding. None had any success.

A few months earlier I'd written Mum and Dad a very long letter, pouring my heart out. I wrote about everything that had happened in the past and said how upset I felt that they weren't coming to the wedding. There was no response, but I sent them a wedding invitation regardless. When it became clear my father wouldn't be there to give me away, Uncle Kevin dropped everything to come to London and walk me down the aisle. This made him very unpopular with my mother, and she didn't talk to him for a long time afterwards.

At one stage leading up to the church wedding, Anthony and I were so disheartened we considered cancelling everything and eloping instead. Then we decided that just because my parents wouldn't be there didn't mean we couldn't have the sort of wedding we were dreaming of, and it was Anthony's first wedding, after all.

I hoped right up to the last minute that my parents would miraculously appear at the wedding, so much so that when they didn't, a day that was meant to be so happy became one of the saddest of my life. The heartbreak I'd felt as I left Perth now seemed complete. I felt like I had lost my family. Every family has its complications, and no one else can ever know what goes on inside a family. Sometimes not even the family members themselves know what's going on. Perhaps that was us: four people not really understanding how our own family worked.

On the day I married Anthony, though, I had the opportunity to start my own family. We were a family of two, for now, but family we were. Amid the grief of losing the family I'd been born into, there was a freedom in having started my own. I'd been posted to the other end of England, to Shropshire, to spend the next eighteen months working as an army divisional legal officer. Anthony was also posted to Shropshire, and there we bought our first house together.

It was a cute little workman's cottage on a fairly large piece of land in a small but very pretty village. We called our nest 'Perth Cottage'.

In Shropshire many of our family and friends lived nearby, which we greatly enjoyed. However, it was difficult for me to adjust to a land-locked county on the border with Wales (as I had grown up on the west coast of Australia and loved to have water nearby) and it felt quite isolated in the end: this farming community turned out to be a bit too quiet and slow paced for two newlyweds!

Working as part of a four-person military legal advisory team, my new job involved providing advice to the chain of command on disciplinary and administrative issues, mostly AWOL and desertion charges, but I also took part in military training and emergency response exercises in order to be prepared in the event of a crisis or a terrorism incident. During my eighteen months in this role I learnt a lot about the command system, military formations and how the army maintained order, discipline and high standards of professionalism – in other words, I gained some insight into how the army dealt with rule-breakers and square pegs in round holes. My divisional base was fairly quiet but there was a strong sense of camaraderie and respect. I was truly made to feel like and accepted as an officer, not just a lawyer in uniform.

By this time the Iraq War was well under way. Anthony had completed his relatively brief deployment to Iraq and increasingly we were hearing news of an Iranian-backed insurgency. The use of roadside bombs, suicide bombs, kidnapping and torture to marginalise the Sunni and the more liberal Muslim people of Iraq was on the rise, particularly in the south, which was under the control of the British.

Out of the blue I received a call from my commanding officer, Lieutenant Colonel Dick Pierce, who told me I'd been selected to become the next UK brigade legal adviser to Iraq. Not only was I the first woman to be given this role; as far as I know I was the most junior officer to have been selected. At the time I'd only recently become an acting major. Dick Pierce didn't want to release me as I was doing so much work within the division, but it was out of his hands. I would spend most of the English winter training with the brigade (often in the snow) before deploying with them as their sole legal adviser in April 2005.

Leaving for Iraq meant leaving my new husband behind in the UK. Anthony and I knew our separation would be very difficult because we'd already done it on a smaller scale, when he'd been sent to Iraq for three months. Now it was my turn to go, and naturally my feelings were mixed. The idea of being apart from Anthony for seven months while I was in Iraq was especially hard. He was my dear husband, but he was also my best friend and my greatest emotional support.

Anthony was very nervous for me, given what he'd experienced in Iraq more than a year earlier. The extreme heat, poor conditions and unpredictable security situation in particular – which had worsened since he was there – were all serious causes for concern.

Before Britain got involved in the Iraq War, my idea of conflict had come from my experience in Northern Ireland.

In other words, war involved an enemy you could see most of the time, even if that enemy was masked. Otherwise, my idea of war, like that of everyone else, was shaped by what I'd seen in the media and in photographs: tanks, bombs, gunfire, and the suffering of innocent victims caught up in the cross-fire and regarded as 'collateral damage'. But here, again, in the images of war that appeared in the media, there was always an identifiable enemy. September 11 had changed everything. As I'd shortly find out, in Iraq as in Afghanistan war meant confronting a faceless enemy, one that travelled among the local community by day and emerged as its true self at night.

Before I left, though, I was preoccupied with something far more personal, which for me was a powerful element in being posted to Iraq: my Muslim heritage. One of the first things I did after receiving news of my deployment was start learning about Islam in earnest, even though I'd begun looking into the religion soon after I joined the army. Aside from anything else, the misinformation and arguments about the Koran's teachings from September 11 onwards had really begun to grate, and I wanted to be better informed. I learnt about the Five Pillars, the ritual of praying, the significance of Mecca and Mohammed as a prophet. As well as reading about Islam, I enrolled in an intensive Arabic language course, because I'd realised that language was also going to be an issue. It has always been important to me to communicate clearly with people, so for me the solution was obvious.

All too soon the departure date arrived. Anthony drove with me to the brigade base in Wiltshire so that we could spend my last night in the UK together. We spent the entire time in each other's arms, just holding each other. It was very emotional, although we both tried to be strong.

The following morning he walked with me to where I was meeting up with some of the other members of the UK brigade also going to Iraq. I wanted Anthony to meet them, so he'd be able to picture faces when I spoke about the people I was working with. He helped me carry my kit, walking with me to the coaches that were taking our group to the military airbase. There was a split second when I thought, *I wonder what would happen if I stayed. I don't know if I can do this. I don't know if my heart is going to bear it, being apart from him for so long.*

Anthony had been wonderful in the days leading up to my departure. He'd reminded me of all the good things I was going to be able to do. He also reminded me that this was what it was all about, this was why we'd joined the armed forces. He'd said he'd be fine – we'd both be fine – and that we'd already been through much worse together. He was my support at a time when I could so easily have gone to pieces, and this helped me switch into officer mode for self-preservation even before we parted, because I knew I had to get a grip.

Nevertheless, all these emotions began hitting me hard as we drove off, and my eyes filled with tears as I looked back through the window at Anthony's figure becoming smaller and smaller until I could see him no longer.

After driving for an hour and a half we arrived at the military airbase at Brize Norton, in Oxfordshire, only to discover that our flight was delayed indefinitely. There was nothing anyone could do about this; we just had to hang around. The pain of leaving Anthony was now enhanced by the realisation we could have had more time together. An hour or so may not seem like much, but when you're about to be sent to a dangerous country, with no guarantee of regular communication with your loved ones, an hour is an eternity.

It was also possible that the delay was a tactic – typical of what I call the 'on the bus, off the bus' factor, which is what they do in the military. I think it's part of the whole psychology they put you through before you leave for a conflict zone. First, they get you away from your loved ones. Then right away they start messing you around, so that you reach a point where you say in huge frustration, 'Oh, let's just get on a plane and get out of here!' Suffice to say, the tactic works.

Eventually we flew out on a Tristar passenger plane operated by the military. I looked out the window as Britain slowly disappeared from view and thought about my wonderful Anthony. Already I missed seeing him and being in his arms.

I tried to imagine what life in Iraq would be like over the coming months. What would the challenges be? What sorts of people would I meet? I knew I could control neither. I was apprehensive, a little scared, and also excited – a whole bundle of mixed emotions. I realised that this posting would be the chance for me to realise many of my career dreams.

What I could control was my reaction to things, whether or not I coped. After everything that had happened in my life thus far, I was sure I would.

CHAPTER NINE

BASRA

We flew to Qatar, then changed planes to a military Hercules and continued on to Basra. Travelling in a Hercules meant we didn't have the luxury of even a quick window glimpse of Iraq before we landed – and our landing was a very steep, fast combat descent. They tell you about the possibility of surface-to-air missiles being fired at planes, and as we plunged down the thought flashed through my mind, *I hope I'm not killed before I set foot on Iraqi soil!*

The heat enveloped us the moment we disembarked. Basra, which is close to Iran and Kuwait, is one of the hottest cities in the world – and it felt like it. Even though I had grown up in the dry heat of Perth, the dry heat of Basra was like an oven. In the peak of summer the temperature would reach over sixty degrees Celsius. My first impression of the country was the blinding colour of the white-brown desert sand that defines this part of the world, and then the sight of hundreds of military rucksacks all looking exactly the same on a trailer, waiting to be sorted. I was a number now – here to serve in an army of many.

Once everyone had managed to find their kit, we were driven south-west to Shaibah, a former Iraqi military airfield the British had turned into a logistics base, which was also the site of our military field hospital.

The next three or four days were spent going through 'acclimatisation', as it's called. We sat in a huge tent getting used to the extreme heat and basic conditions, and listened to a series of lectures and briefings. The first week passed in a blur. Our accommodation was very basic. I shared a tent with twelve to fifteen other women – personnel staff, artillery officers, signallers, clerks and medics – and, like them, had a cot in a little area to myself. I was the only military lawyer in the group.

One of the first challenges, it has to be said, was sharing a small number of portaloos with all the troops. In the extreme heat, the portaloos stank and invariably we all had stomach problems. There were just two blocks of showers to service everyone, which amounted to approximately 100 of us at any one time. So the first few days were a readjustment, to say the least. But everyone deployed in Iraq had to get through this experience before moving on to the British military base at Basra Airport, and I'd been under no illusion that the army involved five-star accommodation. Like everyone else there, I just had to grit my teeth and bear it.

Both the UK brigade and the Multi National Division had their headquarters in the main terminal, which had been converted into a series of offices and operations rooms. Our living accommodation was a short distance away, in a part of the airfield we dubbed 'Waterloo Lines': it was rows and rows of portacabins, with a few toilets and shower blocks, a basic gym, a recreation room and a dining hall.

The man in charge of the UK brigade at that stage was Brigadier Chris Hughes. We'd met before, months earlier, during my pre-deployment training with the brigade back in Britain. An extremely intelligent, measured man, the brigadier was also tall, good-looking and tanned very quickly, so he was as dark as some of the Iraqis. Accordingly, he was known as the 'Dark Prince'. A very cool operator with a lot of charisma, he had a way about him that commanded respect. I was to discover that he communicated well and in a very direct manner. He was also a good listener.

The first time I went into the city of Basra was with Chris. A meeting had been set up with the city's chief judge, Laith Abdul Sammad, who had a lot on his mind, as it would turn out. On this occasion, I didn't dare stick my head out of the Land Rover while we were en route to the meeting; it all seemed too strange, too different – and too dangerous. As time went on I'd become more confident about going about the city and would sit with the window right down in order to get a better view of the place. I'd seen pictures of Basra in its heyday, when it resembled a millionaire's playground with lots of casinos and palaces, but Basra in 2005 was a sad, war-torn place. With its brown, sandy buildings in a complete state of disrepair, as well as the poverty, the smell and the traffic, it wasn't dissimilar to some of the cities I'd seen in my travels.

Basra was dusty, brown and hot – humid at times – and in the city itself there was a constant mixture of smells: open drains, spices, pollution, smoke. Most of the houses had flat roofs and were painted white. There were many impressive buildings and palaces still standing but they were in a state of disrepair. Many had been taken over by the military or the Basra Governorate but that hadn't improved their condition. I could see what a millionaire's playground it would have been – the casino and palaces on the banks of the Shatt Al Arab River were still there but sadly war torn and all but destroyed. Alongside the suffering buildings, there were suffering people living in extreme poverty, some of them in shanty towns close to affluent areas.

Hundreds of miles of arid land separated Basra from its Southern Province neighbouring cities, which were much smaller, more rural and less populated, more run down versions of the bigger city.

The locals didn't seem aggressive; nor did they pay too much attention to us. People didn't stop to look when we drove through; they just kept going about their business. It struck me that they'd lived in a war zone for so long that military vehicles and military personnel had become just a fact of life for them. I could only imagine what it must be like to live that way.

The army called Basra a 'permissive environment', which is military terminology for 'reasonably safe'. In other words, you could get around fairly easily and wouldn't think twice about going to a meeting with someone – you'd get a vehicle and a security detail and set off. This made it easier for us to do our jobs; it also made us feel that our lives were not in danger on a day-to-day basis, so a potentially large source of stress was removed.

My role in Basra was meant to be advising the brigade commander on the legalities of military operations, including rules of engagement and targeting; visiting army units based in Basra to conduct training for troops in rules of engagement and the laws of war; and monitoring search, arrest and detention operations and subsequent interrogations of suspected insurgents. It turned out that it also involved regular meetings with the chief judge and other judges, inspecting prisons and courts, monitoring al-Jamiat police station and conducting human rights 'spot checks' on their detainees. I met with Sunni elders and victims of torture to take their evidence to build their cases.

The day Chris Hughes and I went to meet the chief judge, whom Chris hadn't met before either, we took the usual three Land Rovers. The brigadier was in one and I was in another with our interpreter. In the third were heavily armed soldiers. This was standard procedure, no matter what.

The judge's initial reaction to me – visible surprise that I was a woman – would become very familiar as the weeks passed and I met other Baswaris in authority, sometimes with the brigadier, sometimes on my own. I'd be introduced or introduce myself as Major Rabia, and the first question was always the same: 'Where are you from?' This became an icebreaker.

The meetings were held in order for Chris Hughes to talk with the Baswaris and get to know their concerns. I was there to assist him, but the attention would always start with me because the Iraqis were so curious. When I met the Baswari authorities on my own, it was exactly the same.

I always wore a hijab, or head covering, when I left the base for these meetings, since I was dealing mainly with Iraqi men. This was entirely my decision. The hijab was not something I had ever worn. I had mixed feelings about the perceived suppression of women in Orthodox Muslim societies and questioned whether or not these women had any free will. But when I was with the Iraqis I wore the hijab as a sign of respect. In some more liberal cities the hijab (unlike the niqab, which covers the whole face, or the burqa, which covers the whole body) became a fashion piece.

I also thought wearing the head covering in my meetings with the Iraqis would help with communication, because it showed I had regard for their culture – and regard is an important element in any conversation. The brigadier agreed.

I wore the hijab for the meeting with Judge Laith. He turned out to be a measured man who only opened his mouth to speak if he had something to say. He was polite and gracious as he was introduced to us, but he was distant. He was no doubt aware that British military commanders were only ever there for several months at a time, and so perhaps were not really interested in what was going on in Basra. Each six to seven months Judge Laith would have had to make relationships anew.

When it came time for Judge Laith to speak, he didn't bother with diplomacy. His sentiments, expressed in Arabic, were blunt: 'I'm not interested in your solutions,' he said once the formal pleasantries were over. 'I'm not interested in hearing what you think we want. I'm happy to work with you if you're committed to working with us, to assist us with what we think we need – because there has been enough of the British trying to offer their solutions to our plight, and in some cases this has caused us bigger problems.'

None of the Iraqis were fond of the Americans, but Judge Laith reserved his criticism for the British because of the part they'd played in the formation of Basra's police force, which by now had been thoroughly infiltrated by insurgents.

The problem from the very start of the allied occupation of Iraq was that neither the Americans, nor the Brits – anyone, really – had planned very far ahead. Overthrowing Saddam Hussein had been one thing; the huge task of rebuilding the country quite another. Rash decisions had been made, and many things had been done in too much of a rush. One of the gravest mistakes in Basra, as in Baghdad, was to recruit an Iraqi police service quickly and poorly, as a second priority to rebuilding the Iraqi Army.

There had been no proper officer selection process; I think people were even paid to join. So you got the corrupt, the criminals and the insurgents, as well as those who were easy prey for their radical and violent colleagues. In other words, most of the people in the police force were either poorly qualified or corrupt, or they were insurgents and terrorists. The Basra police service was now the biggest problem in the region.

At every meeting I'd go on to attend – whether it was with the governor of Basra or the chief judge – there was a common cry from the Iraqis present: 'If you want to help us, sort out the police service. Help us provide security for our judges so they don't feel afraid to return to the courts. Help us with rebuilding our courts. It's all about security.'

No one was exaggerating the situation, or what the Iraqis were up against. The Jaish al-Mahdi insurgents – who used their police uniforms as a cover to carry out surveillance on locals during the day – operated in similar fashion to the Taliban in Afghanistan. They targeted women going to university, women who weren't wearing the hijab, and both men and women who were continuing to lead a liberal life – which is what Basra had once been known for.

It may be a disquieting, uncomfortable fact for many Westerners, but Iraq had been quite liberal under Saddam Hussein's Sunni regime – liberal in the sense that even though Saddam was a monster and did horrific things to his people, Iraqis were able to lead a relatively free life as long as they toed his line. It was not a totalitarian regime in the same sense as North Korea is still; nor did it resemble the Islamic fundamentalism and repression that were forced upon many Iraqis after Saddam was overthrown.

Judge Laith's frustration with the British was understandable. At night, insurgents in police uniforms were kidnapping, beating, raping and killing the men and women they'd targeted. The British Army and other Coalition forces were supposedly in Iraq to help the country rebuild itself after the end of a regime that very Coalition had helped topple. Certain responsibilities go along with marching into someone else's country and telling them how to run it – helping to ensure law and order is one of them.

Chris Hughes didn't share his thoughts with me after we left our first meeting with the judge. He was quite a private man who kept himself to himself. As time went on, though, Chris admitted to me that he wanted to get stuck in and sort out the police force by arresting and detaining the insurgents. What he didn't say – couldn't say – was that he was hamstrung politically. There were generals above him and people at Divisional Headquarters, as well as in the British Government, who very much wanted us to tread quietly, despite the reality of the situation in Basra. So, as much as he might have wanted to help, he either couldn't do so or couldn't be seen to be doing so.

The British Government was desperate to keep a lid on what was happening. Nobody in government wanted the British public to find out how the police force we'd created was dominated by insurgents and killers who were working against us and whom neither the British nor the Iraqi authorities were able to control. The lack of political will – though not necessarily a lack of military will – on the part of the British to allow us to do anything decisive had only added to the problem faced every day by the people of Basra and the British forces who were stationed there to help them.

The Basra Governorate and a lot of the Sunni clerics were extremely frustrated about this situation, and this became a conflict for me, too. I'd visited countries where the authorities were corrupt or had unlimited control and power over citizens who felt intimidated and powerless. My legal training had taught me to think rather than just follow orders. I could see the bigger picture and could appreciate and understand the message we were constantly receiving loud and clear from the Iraqis: 'You've created this problem. You came here and overthrew Saddam. Great. Thank you. But all the problems we're experiencing now have come from your actions. So what are you going to do about it?'

In all honesty, I think the British authorities were genuinely concerned that if we admitted we'd gone into Iraq too quickly, and without a plan, this would play into Iran's hands, since it was becoming increasingly clear that Iran was backing and fuelling a lot of the violence in Basra. Intelligence suggested that Iran was financing Muqtada al-Sadr, and that Iranian weapons and technology were being used by Jaish al-Mahdi and Sadr's followers. In other words, if London had given the okay for the British forces to go in hard and tackle the situation, there would have been further reaction from Iran – which had not been a friend of the UK or the US for a very long time – and the violence would only escalate. I think Chris Hughes would agree if I said that for the entire time he was the commander in Basra politically he operated in Basra with one arm tied behind his back. He was sent there to do a job he was then not permitted to do.

It was quite obvious that the British forces were there – we were highly visible. For the people of Basra to know we'd helped create this police force that was causing them so many problems but then weren't doing anything to stop that force's violence and corruption must have made them distrust us. How could they ever believe us if we promised anything? How could I, as a lawyer, do my job effectively if the people I was dealing with thought that all we did was cause problems?

It was a very difficult situation, and one that required us all to be tremendously mindful of how we dealt with the Iraqis. I had to deal with them authentically – I needed to be able to tell them the truth. In many ways, it felt as though this was work I'd spent my life preparing to do and wanting to do. Instead of seeing it as a challenge, I saw it as a chance: a chance to help people, to protect them – to put my heart on the line, in a way. I'd have many, many chances to do just that.

CHAPTER TEN

DESPICABLE ACTS AND
COURAGEOUS VICTIMS

Judge Laith's strong words to Brigadier Hughes left us in no doubt that there were projects he wanted us to get onto if the situation in Basra was to improve under the British.

One project that was started by my predecessors and was consistent with Judge Laith's priorities was the formation of joint British and Iraqi teams attached to every court in all the provinces in southern Iraq. The teams were there to provide security, and help local judges and their staff with the running of the courts. They also had to make sure everyone who'd been arrested and detained went through the court system, and that the courts were secure. It was a huge task, and one I started coordinating straight away. I had the teams report back to me on a weekly basis to ensure the courts were running smoothly and any issues were being addressed.

As I got to know Judge Laith better, and he started to trust me and see how I got things done by building relationships with the Iraqis as well as the allied forces, he started asking for more of my help. Soon I was assisting the British Government, the Iraqi Government and the International Red Cross by making prison visits to inspect the human rights situation – with the aim of ensuring the prisoners' basic human rights, as set out by the Red Cross, were being met.

The brigadier and I had already discovered that Basra had no prison escort service. There was literally no way of taking people who'd been arrested and detained to court. There was no one to escort them, either. We found out about this hopeless state of affairs after visiting Basra's two main prisons – visits that left us both in shock.

The prisons were horrific, crumbling places with no basic facilities to speak of, not even proper sanitation. The prisoners were living in total squalor. There were even women with children in prison, and the female prisons were so overcrowded that the authorities had put women into dedicated areas inside male prisons. Many of the prisoners, both male and female, were there on trumped-up charges. They'd never been to court and were being held on what we would understand as remand – except it was indefinite remand.

There were prisoners who were well educated and had been living a liberated style of life, which of course was anathema to the Shiite fundamentalists. There were teachers, lawyers and former politicians trapped inside those prisons, and most of the time I couldn't work out what their 'crimes' were – except when it was obvious that they, too, had been part of a liberal Iraq. Occasionally I'd come across people who'd say in Arabic,

'God bless you. Please help us.' But they were few and far between. I got a sense that most of the prisoners had seen so many white people in uniforms come through that they no longer had any hope something would be done for them.

Many prisoners were poor Sunnis. I couldn't get a sense of the reason for the great numbers of imprisoned Sunnis, though. Maybe it was simply because, being poor, they had no way to pay bribes or call on influential people on the outside to help free them. If this really was the case, then the extremists were simply using them to send a message of intimidation to the rest of the community.

Some people had been locked away for years and never had their cases heard. The brigadier and I found ourselves constantly asking prison staff why, although we were actually asking it about everything we saw: the squalor, the appalling conditions, the fact that people had never had their cases heard in court – if, indeed, there was any substance to their cases. The answer was always the same: 'Money. We don't have enough money for food, for plumbing, for sewerage. That's the situation. If you could help us … We just don't have the facilities to get these people to court.'

I tried to work out if this was an excuse or the reality, but after doing a great deal more research, I realised it truly was the reality. There was no prison escort service as we would understand it, and no way, it seemed, that the people running Basra's prison system could organise one. Money wasn't the problem – rather, the problem was administrative: the money wasn't getting to the places where it was needed. Money was given to the government and the Governorate of the provinces, who decided how and to whom it would be distributed. Insurgents had a lot of control and had infiltrated high levels of government and administration.

Even so, just to make sure no one could use the lack of this service as an excuse for why people weren't getting justice, I set about trying to find out if it was possible to obtain funding to buy a couple of vehicles and train some of the prison guards to double up as prisoner escorts. Judge Laith supported this work from the start and encouraged me to keep at it. In time, we were able to achieve what Basra had never had: a proper prison escort service. It began operating just before I left Iraq at the end of my tour.

Going into the prisons was a revelation, but it was just the start of a journey into Basra's heart of darkness. The brigadier had started holding meetings with elders from the Sunni community, and he asked me to attend them. Life for many Sunnis in Iraq had become a nightmare after Saddam was overthrown and the Shiite majority rose to power. I met people who told me horrific stories of the treatment they'd suffered at the hands of the police. The Sunni elders asked me to help get them justice. Even if they hadn't asked, I'd have done everything I could for these people. The brigadier was more than happy for me to go ahead. 'Tell me what you need and carry on,' he said. My needs were simple: a security detail to come with me when I met the victims to take their statements, an interpreter and a tape recorder.

It wasn't long before I became involved in preparing a class action for the Iraq Central Criminal Court in Baghdad against the officers who'd allegedly tortured and murdered more than 300 Sunni Iraqi men in Basra alone during the previous two years. Taking on this class action would normally have been the job of the Red Cross, Amnesty International or another NGO, but they didn't have a presence in Basra and weren't prepared to go to the places and speak to the people necessary to building the case. There was no automatic jurisdiction for a British lawyer to appear in an Iraqi court, so the plan was that once the case had been prepared, an Iraqi lawyer would be engaged and briefed to take over.

Right from the start, I explained to the Sunnis that if they wanted justice, it would have to be through the court system. Initially they weren't keen on this idea because all they'd ever known was rough justice, and I think they expected we could just imprison their torturers without due process. We could develop a class action, I emphasised, but explained that we would have to take it right away from Basra to the Central Criminal Court in Baghdad, to ensure impartiality and to protect them.

I left Iraq before the class action went to court, so I do not know the outcome. I expect that the civil unrest that took over after the Jamiat incident would have scared off some of the victims.

Eventually, these very damaged men placed their trust in me. There was a bit of reluctance from some of the torture victims who'd survived their treatment, as they were understandably paranoid about having their identities known. I reassured them that we'd keep their identities secret, and said it was imperative for us to carry on with our plan. Much later on, once I had all the statements, I went to Baghdad with Chris Hughes to meet with the chief justice of Iraq. I was able to secure his agreement to hear this case and to protect the identities of all the victims, which had never been done before in an Iraqi court.

I also met many of the families of Iraqi men and women who'd been kidnapped and killed by Captain Jaffar, the head of the SCU run out of al-Jamiat, and his men. They told me how men dressed in police uniforms would raid their homes or arrive at their places of work and drag their relatives away. Some of the 'disappeared' were plucked from their studies at university. Many days or weeks later the body of a brother who'd been taken, or a sister, a wife, a husband or even a child, would turn up on the outskirts of the city – most of them carrying the unmistakeable signs of torture and beatings.

Occasionally, the families would hear that their loved ones were being detained somewhere. They weren't allowed to see them or to visit them – which in itself is a form of torture. You can imagine the anguish these families went through as they pictured the horrors their parents, siblings, husbands, wives, and even sometimes children were suffering. Iraqis are very proud, very private people, and because of my own family history I could relate to them culturally – Muslim communities are not necessarily so different around the world. To see men and women – and particularly the men – weeping as they told me these stories was heartbreaking.

I was enormously moved that they were telling me the stories they were too scared to tell anyone else. They no longer knew who to trust, which was hardly a surprise in

Basra at that time. Even the governor of Basra was rumoured to be an insurgency sympathiser. So I was aware that I was being entrusted with something very precious: their truth, and also their dignity. They were relying on me to preserve one by telling the other. It could have been a burden, but instead it felt like a privilege. How lucky I'd been in my own life – to grow up in a country that looked after its citizens, to be able to go to university and become a lawyer so that I could do this work, to be able to travel around the world in order to find the opportunity that brought me here. Now I had the chance to use the great fortune of my own life to help these people who had none.

It was important for me to hear each of their stories. People described how they'd been hung upside down and beaten ferociously on the soles of their feet until there was only bloody, raw flesh left; or had wires attached to their teeth, their toes, their fingers and their genitals before being given atrocious electric shocks.

One young man in particular stays in my mind. He told me how he was hung upside down for hours before he was beaten ferociously and given electrical torture. There was a softness and a vulnerability about him, and I think he stays in my memory so strongly because he was the first torture victim I met. That and the fact that he was so young he could barely grow a full moustache. His father had been involved in local politics, and he was picked up because of his father's activities. I'm fairly certain he suffered a second round of torture so that his mother and sisters wouldn't be taken in for similar treatment. A lot of the men I met endured all this in the hope that at least the women in their family would be protected. Some were, some weren't. I only spoke to male victims of torture. I think it was a step too far, culturally and emotionally, for the women to describe what had been done to them, even to another woman.

Listening to what these people had been through had a huge effect on me. Privately, I think I shed tears – it's hard to remember whether I did or not, because I was so preoccupied with trying to help them, and now, years later, it's my memories of them, not my own reactions, that come back.

Two of the Iraqis I met in particular I consider very special. I learnt a lot from both and will never forget them. One was a young woman called Nour al Khal. It was through Nour that I gained the strongest sense of what daily life for liberal Iraqis had become after members of the Jaish al-Mahdi began terrorising the city. Nour told me in much greater detail about the number of Sunnis who'd been killed or tortured, and what the Jaish al-Mahdi did to people after snatching them from their houses.

We met after she sought me out. She appeared one day outside the rear gate at Basra Airport. As I learnt later, she'd travelled part of the distance by car and had walked the rest of the way. The security staff sent through a message: there was a local woman at the gate asking if she could speak to me. They were initially suspicious and thought she was a journalist but eventually Nour was let in. She turned out to be a very articulate woman, probably in her mid-twenties, who spoke excellent English. I think she had jeans on the first time we met, as well as a tunic and hijab, and she came across as extremely intelligent and brave.

'This is what has become of Basra. We're now forced to wear the hijab for our own protection,' she said scathingly once we'd sat down and were talking. She was quick to point out that she'd never worn a hijab in the past. Nour was very resentful that she'd lost so much freedom under the new Iraq controlled by the Shiite radicals. 'I used to enjoy wearing make-up and painting my nails. I can't do any of that now,' she added.

She wore a wedding ring for 'protection', although she wasn't married. According to Iraqi culture, Nour was quite old to be unmarried, but this didn't concern her. She had a degree in English from Basra University and was a professional interpreter, but after the Saddam regime fell, it was no longer safe for her to go out to work. Many professional women in Iraq were in the same situation. Nour became an interpreter for an American journalist called Steven Vincent, and the two of them had struck up a friendship.

Nour was well aware that she was putting her life at risk by working with Steven – and even more so by coming to see me. But she said she'd rather die knowing that at least she'd passed on information and tried to help her people rather than done nothing at all. It turned out she'd heard about me through her contacts.

'I'm talking to you because I'm hoping you might be able to help us, or at least I'm hoping you can do something with whatever information I can give you,' she said.

It was a Friday – Prayer Day – when we first met. Nour thought she'd be less visible coming to the base when most people were in the mosque, although of course there was no way her visit to the base could have passed unnoticed. We had Iraqi security forces helping defend the base, as well as Iraqi civilian security contractors, and the reality was you never knew who was trustworthy. In all likelihood some of the locals working at the base were informants for Jaish al-Mahdi.

Seeking me out took great courage on Nour's part. She was obviously committed to doing something to help change the security situation in Basra. I found her inspiring and later, after she'd left, I told the brigadier about her and suggested the two of them meet when she next came to see me. He did come to one of my several meetings with Nour and he agreed afterwards that she was a reliable and trustworthy source.

As well as providing information about police torture and murder victims, she suggested ways of finding the survivors. She also knew about the special cell at the Jamiat police station I'd just found out about and would eventually see for myself. She knew about the various methods of torture used by the police. And she knew about Captain Jaffar. In short, Nour put flesh on the bones of the intelligence we already had. She also confirmed that the governor was a Shiite radical sympathiser and wasn't to be trusted.

But in the time we spent together, Nour and I also talked as two women from Muslim backgrounds. We both hated the way Islam was being used as an excuse for violence and persecution. We didn't speak in intimate detail about the teachings or practice of Islam, although we agreed that as human beings there was far more that should bind Muslims,

Christians and Jews together – indeed, people from all religions – than should separate them. From time to time, we discussed our respective lives: hers as a modern woman in an Islamic country, and mine as a woman in a modern, non-Islamic country.

It wasn't so much a friendship between Nour and me as an understanding. There was affection, though, and I know that because just thinking about her even now makes me emotional. She was someone I greatly admired, and at the end of our meetings we'd always embrace while I'd say in Arabic, 'God bless and see you soon.'

I knew that as soon as she stepped outside the gates, she was at risk again. And three months after Nour first turned up at the gates of the base, an intelligence report came in to headquarters. Nour and Steven Vincent had been snatched. Witnesses said the pair had been walking along a street in Basra when they were grabbed by men in police uniforms and forced into a car. I knew they'd both been receiving death threats, which made the news of their disappearance even worse. For several days we heard nothing more. I was so worried for Nour, for them both.

It was incredibly hard not to be able to help search for her – not only was this not my role, but it had become increasingly dangerous for us to leave the base. The security situation had begun to deteriorate dramatically and the violence we were increasingly experiencing from the insurgents meant that our movements were drastically curtailed. Then Steven's body was found. He'd been shot in the back of the head. Nour was discovered soon afterwards, lying not far from Steven's body. She'd been badly beaten, and they'd shot her three times. Incredibly, she'd survived.

I immediately asked our intelligence people to keep me fully informed about what was happening, and learnt that after receiving medical treatment Nour had been transferred to a hospital in Baghdad. Eventually she was taken out of Iraq by the allied forces, and she now lives in America. She was sponsored there by Steven Vincent's widow.

The other Iraqi I admired deeply was a man called Assaf Al Nahi, who was Judge Laith's associate. Assaf had been involved with the British military before I arrived in Basra and had worked with my predecessors, so in a way he was assigned to me. But presumably because of my background, Assaf had more in common with me than he'd had with my predecessors, and I think that as a result our working relationship was twice as productive.

We became friends, and I met his wife and their little boy after he brought them out to see me at the base. It was Assaf who introduced the brigadier and me to Judge Laith and helped me with some of the work I was doing in the courts. He also provided me with valuable and actionable intelligence about the activities of the Basra Murder Squad.

On one occasion he phoned to say that he was outside the base and needed to see me straight away. I arranged for him to be escorted to my office, where I dropped everything to talk with him. With the widest smile on his face he said he and his wife had just come back from a holiday and he'd brought me a gift. He then proudly presented me with a beautifully wrapped red top and said he hoped I'd wear it once I'd returned to the UK – and think of them whenever I did so.

Assaf was murdered by Jaish al-Mahdi killers the year after I left Iraq. I understand that his wife, who was pregnant when he died, had their second child soon afterwards. I often picture her with the little fellow and the baby, both growing up now without their father. All Assaf had ever wanted was to help his people, keep his family safe and progress further with his legal career, much like me.

I often thought it was just as well, in my role as the brigadier's legal adviser, that I was working alone and had a lot of autonomy, because as I felt increasingly more empathy for people like Nour and Assaf, I was beginning to feel a little detached and, at times, quite frustrated with some of my military colleagues.

It wasn't their fault they weren't able to spend the same sort of time with the Iraqi people, or empathise with their plight in the way I could. But my frustration grew with the way some of my colleagues maintained a very British, colonialist attitude towards the Iraqis. I don't really include the rank-and-file soldiers here. They were young, they were over there to do a job, and those I spoke to didn't think too deeply about the lives of the Iraqis post-Saddam. I guess they couldn't afford to get caught up in the emotion of it all. Usually they simply referred to Iraqis as 'ragheads'.

It was the 'Hoorah Henrys' among the officers who annoyed me the most – those who'd led a very privileged life in the UK and had never been exposed to ordinary Iraqis. They didn't see any of these people as human beings they could relate to; those who were tortured and murdered were just 'civilian casualties' in their minds. I did try to share with most of my colleagues some of the insights I'd gained into the lives of Iraqis. Some key people did want to hear what was happening. I could see that they sympathised and really thought about what I told them. Chris Hughes was one of them. As steely, cool and intimidating as he was – both as a man and as a commander – I could see that he was listening and digesting everything I said. Our padre, Cole Maynard, was another I could talk to in depth.

In a way I was almost living in a universe parallel to that of my military colleagues, because while they were immersing themselves in army and military business I was out in Basra talking with, helping and being informed by locals. And as I immersed myself more and more in the lives of the people I was serving, I increasingly began to concentrate my energy, my heart and my efforts on them.

I was invited into people's homes, which was an incredible privilege – I realised how much trust was being placed in me just with the act of the invitation. A lot of the men I worked with wanted to introduce me to their wives and children. Not only were they showing affection and hospitality towards me but great bravery to even consider putting themselves at such risk. The pity of it was that I couldn't possibly accept their courageous and kind invitations for that very reason. Nonetheless, their generosity of spirit really touched me.

Something else deeply affected me as well. I'd grown up with a Muslim father who'd done everything to distance himself from his Islamic identity in order to fit in. In turn,

I'd done the same. But once I got to Basra and got to know so many well-educated, passionate, inspiring people, I felt nothing but regret that I hadn't before been exposed to such positive examples of the Muslim faith. As a result I began to feel much closer to my religion and truly willing to allow Islam to be a part of my identity. Even though I don't practise Islam I identify myself as having Islamic roots and heritage, and I became proud that being Muslim was a part of who I am. I met some incredible people in Basra whom I will hold up all my life as the true image of Islam. I felt inadequate that I didn't know more, and was almost apologetic when I spent time with Iraqis.

Helping the people of Basra obtain justice became my driving obsession. Perhaps it was partly my way of making up for lost time. My strong sense of duty to the Iraqis became the emotion I was running on. And I use that word 'duty' deliberately. I felt I had dual duties: one to the British forces and the British Government that had sent me to Iraq, the other to the Iraqis. And, to be honest, my sense of duty to the Iraqis was beginning to feel stronger at times than my sense of duty to the military.

My parents met in the skies in the late 1960s when my dad was a purser with Air India and my mother a tour guide. They eloped to Perth and married in a civil ceremony in 1970, with just a few friends around them.

I was born in King Edward Hospital, Subiaco, in 1971. I was named after my father's beloved mother. Rabia means 'spring' in Arabic.

Me with Angus, my Uncle Kevin's dog and one of my first Aussie friends! At kindergarten I stuck out with my good manners and strong English accent. I had dark skin, dark hair and big blue eyes among a crop of largely Anglo kids.

TOP: Me with my parents and my brother Adam (born in 1979). Perth in the 1970s was small and quite isolated from the rest of Australia and there were few foreigners. My father faced prejudice almost every day.

LEFT: I loved my high-school years at Penrhos College. Not only was I named school captain in my final year but I met Queen Elizabeth II at a Commonwealth Youth Tea Party during her bicentenary visit to Perth in 1988.

OPPOSITE: During my time at uni, my relationship with my parents disintegrated but I blossomed in the intellectually stimulating environment. After studying for an Arts degree, I pursued Law. I knew I wanted to spend my life helping people who were powerless.

While living in England, I attended a lecture given by retired British army officer, Colonel John Blashford-Snell, the founder of the Royal Scientific Exploration Society. He was looking for volunteers to join the 1999 Kota Mama Expedition and keen for an adventure, I signed up.

Some of the people on the expedition were members of the British Armed Forces and I became very good friends with one person in particular, a Royal Engineer and former bomb disposal officer called Nathan Arnison. He was the one who suggested I join the army as a legal officer.

I participated in various community aid projects, carried out wildlife conservation tasks and met with tribal elders to discuss means of restoring law and order within their communities to reduce tensions between their tribes and their governments.

In March 2001, I submitted an application for a commission with the British Army Legal Services (ALS) and in September, I was formerly commissioned as a captain. Through the army I hoped to work in the area of international humanitarian law and to help people on a larger scale.

LEFT: Time for some fun! Thirtieth birthday celebrations with good friends at my 'Popstars' themed party in West London, just prior to deploying to Northern Ireland in November 2001.

OPPOSITE: Anthony and I married in London in July 2004, at St Clement Danes, Strand in London. I was devastated when my parents declined to attend our wedding. I hoped right up to the last minute that they might appear, but they didn't.

I met my husband Anthony when he was an officer in the Royal Air Force. We were stationed at the same RAF base in Uxbridge, near London, where Anthony was an air traffic controller. This photo was taken at Uxbridge in May 2003 not long after we started dating.

Even though I had grown up in the dry heat of Perth, Basra felt like an oven. Upon arrival, I shared a tent with twelve to fifteen other women. All I had was a cot in a little area to myself. I was the only military lawyer in the group.

Here I am as the sole UK brigade legal adviser with the UK, Australian and Danish Military legal officers that made up the Multi National Division South East legal contingent in Basra in 2005.

Me with UK civilian and military police advisers and members of the court liaison teams, in Basra, August 2005. I had a good relationship with all of these people and we worked hard together to ensure a better standard of training was provided to local police officers so the courts in Southern Iraq were able to function again.

Me at Basra Palace with Brigadier John Lorimer and elders from the Sunni community. These two Sunni elders sought my help with the class action against members of the Serious Crimes Unit who had been kidnapping, torturing and murdering local Sunnis.

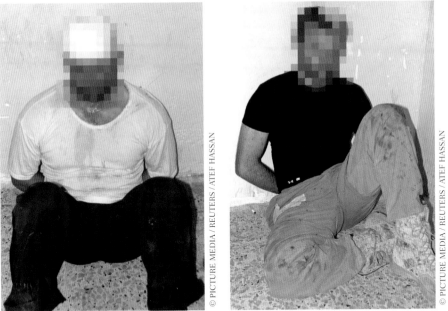

© PICTURE MEDIA / REUTERS / ATEF HASSAN

© PICTURE MEDIA / REUTERS / ATEF HASSAN

ABOVE (BOTH): Basra, 19 September 2005. Two SAS soldiers, pseudonyms Ed and Di, were involved in a surveillance operation when they were spotted by locals who alerted the police. Ed and Di were captured at a checkpoint after they exchanged gunfire with police. They were taken to the notorious al-Jamiat prison, where I was called in to negotiate their release.

AFP / GETTY IMAGES

The Jamiat police station is an extremely dangerous place for any member of the British Army. It's the headquarters of the Serious Crimes Unit, which local Iraqis refer to – without joking – as the 'Murder Squad'.

Just as Judge Raghib and I were about to reach an agreement for the release of Di and Ed, rocket-propelled grenades and petrol bombs exploded outside al-Jamiat. The rampaging crowds were attempting to storm the building.

A British soldier makes his way out of a burning Warrior fighting vehicle during the clash.

Me sitting at my desk in my office at UK Brigade HQ, Basra, September 2005. I'd just come out of hospital following a knee injury that I sustained on the way back from giving evidence at the Iraqi inquiry into the Jamiat incident.

At the same time as James Woodham received the Miltary Cross, I was awarded a Queen's Commendation for Valuable Service. I thought it was for al-Jamiat but then I discovered it was for the human rights work I'd been doing in Basra. My anger at having become a ghost in the Jamiat affair grew and I decided to take action.

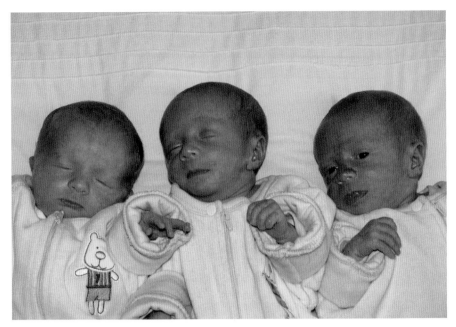

At the beginning of 2008, Anthony and I were ecstatic to discover we were expecting triplets! There was a brief time of worry when Oscar and Noah suffered from twin-to-twin transfusion syndrome, which can have dangerous complications. Thankfully the condition righted itself.

It was motherhood, not Iraqi insurgents, which turned me into a lioness overnight. Within seconds after birth though, Aaron, Noah and Oscar were whisked away to the neonatal intensive care unit. The first of my babies that I held was Oscar, two days after the boys were born.

COURTESY OF VENTURE PHOTOGRAPHY

Anthony is my rock. During the harrowing days of the court case against the British army, he stood by me and gave me strength. Now he plays a hands-on role as a partner to me and parent to our sons. We are an invincible couple.

KARIN CALVERT / NEWSPIX

What never wavers in me is my dedication to duty, whether it's duty to my job or duty to my family. I need both. And as a working mother, I can be committed to both parts of my life.

Ultimately, I do not know how to live if I am not treating others equally. The application of justice is some of the hardest work we will undertake as a society. But it's the most important. I have no regrets that I stood up and challenged the unjust treatment I received.

CHAPTER ELEVEN

CAPTAIN JAFFAR AND THE BASRA MURDER SQUAD

I first visited al-Jamiat police station within weeks of arriving in Basra. By then I'd been shown a lot of the intelligence on the police officers there, and I knew I'd probably meet Captain Jaffar when I visited. Jaffar was notorious, and not just among the British forces – the people of Basra knew all about him too. So I was fairly apprehensive as we left base.

Chris Hughes came with me, and as soon as we arrived at al-Jamiat we were taken to see Colonel Ali al-Sewan, the head of the DIA. After some general discussion in his office, the colonel went with us into the neighbouring compound, where we were introduced to the police who worked for the SCU. That is, they were Jaffar's men. Jaffar was there too.

The leader of the Basra Murder Squad – as the SCU was known – turned out to be a fairly short, stocky man with a sleek, well-groomed moustache. He was charming and very cordial. When he was introduced to me, he smiled and asked the usual question: 'Ah, Rabia, a Muslim name. What's your background?'

I played the game and was charming back, because it was necessary for me to develop a relationship with this man. Jaffar held a lot of the information I needed, and I'd pretty much come to terms with the fact that I'd have to court the enemy – for a time, anyway. I don't think he was necessarily aware that I was working on a class action for Sunni victims of torture and murder. All Jaffar knew for sure was that I was assisting the British Government, the Iraqi Government and the Red Cross by carrying out human rights visits to police stations and prisons. He may well have had spies reporting back to him, and probably would have known we were in contact with representatives of the Sunni community. But that was all.

Without going into too much detail, we were always very careful about how, where and when we would meet the torture victims to obtain statements. We would take different routes, and I'd always go with a security detail. Even with these precautions, however, some of the Sunni elders were visited and arrested by Jaffar's men after our sessions. We had to negotiate for their release and a few were understandably scared of meeting with us again. I lost the support of some of the elders as a result.

My visits to the Jamiat became a regular part of my routine, and through all of my dealings with Jaffar, his charm never let up. As a lawyer carrying out spot checks on the SCU's detention cells, I also performed a monitoring role by making sure prisoners and those on remand were being treated humanely. I made it my business to ensure the SCU officers knew I was keeping a close eye on them. And because I'd developed good relationships with the Iraqi authorities, the British Army sometimes asked me to gather intelligence on Jaffar's thugs.

Our intelligence on the SCU officers had revealed that they regularly attended night meetings in various houses belonging to Jaish al-Mahdi members. We knew that they all got together to plan operations, that Jaffar was also at these meetings, and that he was behind many of the roadside bombs that had killed so many people. His name had also been mentioned as one of those who'd been torturing, kidnapping and killing local Iraqis. In short, we kept hearing his name over and over again.

During that first meeting, the brigadier said he wanted a tour around the complex. Jaffar reluctantly obliged. We knew, of course, that a lot of the torture took place in their so-called interrogation rooms. They allowed us to have a look in these rooms during the tour and we could see where the wires used for electrical torture had been pulled out of light sockets.

I knew what questions to ask them – 'Do you have prisoners here? Where are you holding them? Where are your cells?' – and they eventually admitted they were holding some people. I had to ask the questions, but I also took the answers I was given with a grain of salt.

I wasn't taken to see the cells on the first tour. That didn't happen until my third or fourth visit to the Jamiat, which is when I first saw the particularly awful cell in which they were holding more than 200 men. Sunni elders, and Nour and Assaf had already told me about this cell. It was probably smaller than a very small school hall – about twenty metres by fifteen metres – with cold, dirty cement floors and walls in a state of semi-collapse. There was a putrid smell. I think there was just one open drop toilet behind a makeshift screen.

From the very first time I was allowed access, without exception the police would go in first and spend maybe ten minutes out of sight. I assumed they were doing a quick clean-up and threatening the prisoners to prevent them speaking to me. I always asked the police the same questions: 'How long have these people been here? What are they accused of? When will they be going to court?' The answers were always evasive.

By the time I walked into the cell, all these poor people would be seated or kneeling in rows with their heads down. They wouldn't make eye contact with me. There was row after row of them, and I'd say nearly all of them were Sunnis. It was a sight I'd never imagined before and hope to never see again: so many defeated people, detained for no good reason anyone could identify, paying a price simply for being who they were.

I didn't know their identities the first time I went in. Occasionally I stopped and spoke to some of them, asking how they were and how long they'd been there. They were too scared to answer, so I stopped.

Afterwards, I'd arrange separate meetings with the Sunni elders to find out more about the men being kept in that cell, and I'd ask what they looked like and whether they had other family members with them. Once I had a quick description or a photograph, I knew who to look for on another of these spot visits and would go straight to talk to the ones I'd been told had been in there for years. I could only do this when an opportunity presented itself, which was one of the reasons I'd take Major James Woodham or one of the men from the surveillance unit he headed to distract the police by talking to them separately just outside the cell.

As a result of these visits, probably up to about thirty of the prisoners were either released or taken to court to answer the charges against them. It turned out many were in prison under the guise of 'terrorism', which basically meant they'd questioned or challenged the Shiite fundamentalist regime.

I never did end up having a one-to-one conversation with Jaffar during these visits. I asked him the odd question about the people in that cell, such as what they'd been charged with, but he always made sure we were never alone together so I couldn't question him in detail about anything. Occasionally I saw him at meetings with Basra's Governorate, at the Old State and Provincial Buildings in the city, which was also how we concluded that he held considerable power. Otherwise, what would a captain in the Iraqi Police Service be doing at meetings with the governor?

A lot of the work I was doing was on behalf of a human rights barrister on the staff of the British consul in Basra, a woman called Olivia Holdsworth. Olivia's brief was to gather information about human rights abuses and report back to the British Government and non-government organisations such as the Red Cross. She was living with the rest of the consular staff in relative luxury at Basra Palace, the sort of place that was ideal for the garden parties regularly thrown there by the consul general. I only went to one such party and left wondering what the Iraqi guests thought about the strange rituals they'd witnessed that harked back to the days of the British Empire: string quartets, military bands, strawberries and canapés. In the middle of a place that was still recovering from a war, it all seemed so bizarre.

Right from our first meeting, Olivia asked me to work closely with her, since it was clear I was able to go to places and speak to people she couldn't access, thanks to my position, my background, my name and my (limited) Arabic. When she returned to the UK, however, I was working on my own, sometimes up to sixteen hours a day, seven days a week. There was just so much to be done.

I think my passion, commitment and hard work made a big impression on Chris Hughes and this was why he gave me so much support. It helped, of course, that I was able to go out and meet the people I needed to talk to, because up until about August the so-called permissive environment, which allowed me the freedom to keep doing what I was doing, remained intact. So it was extremely unfortunate when, around the time of the London bombings, Chris was recalled to London to take up his new appointment at the Ministry of Defence and the security situation in the city got very bad, very fast, just before he went back.

This was the start of a horrific period in Basra when new, more powerful armour-piercing roadside bombs using sophisticated infrared technology that was being shipped over from

Iran began killing many more of our soldiers. When Brigadier John Lorimer arrived to replace Chris Hughes, he decided it was high time to arrest Ahmed al-Fartusi, the leader of Jaish al-Mahdi in southern Iraq.

Fartusi's arrest was the opening gambit from the new commander, a declaration that he was going to run things differently. A couple of days later, Ed and Di ran into a police roadblock. And I was sent into the Jamiat.

CHAPTER TWELVE

AL-JAMIAT PART 2

James Woodham and I had gone to the Jamiat to try to free our two Special Forces soldiers Ed and Di. I'd almost succeeded in freeing them when mayhem erupted outside the compound and before we knew it a crazed man was pointing an AK47 at us.

I looked the man in the eyes – by instinct rather than design, since everything seemed to be happening in slow motion. I had time to think, *If this bastard is going to kill me, I'm going to look him in the eyes while he does it.* I took a breath and held his gaze. And I felt something – a quality, I realised in a flash, I'd always possessed. At nine, I was too young to know it. At nineteen, I'd begun to test its limits. Now, at thirty-three, with an AK47 pointed at my head, I knew its name.

Defiance.

I'm a lawyer. I was neither a steely, highly trained killing machine nor a battle-hardened soldier. I'd been sent into this high-risk situation at the Jamiat for my brain, my negotiating ability and, I guess, my humanity and the fact that I'd earned the trust of these people and fostered good relations with some of them. When horrific things had happened in Iraq – when I'd heard heartbreaking stories and been shown the scars left by torture or seen babies imprisoned with their mothers in filthy, overcrowded prisons – I'd been able to deal with it coolly and calmly, and keep my wits about me.

But right there, in that room, in front of those leering men and that maniac with an assault rifle, I shocked myself. I realised, in that instant, that I could deal with anything. I could feel fear and not capitulate to it. I could be alone and strong with it. I could defy anyone who threatened me.

I continued to hold the gunman's gaze.

Suddenly, Captain Jaffar rushed forward and wrestled the man to the floor, helped by some of his men. They dragged the would-be assassin out of the room – and that was the last we saw of him.

I was stunned. I perhaps said something to James but I can't remember now. I know I became aware of my heart beating – hard – and a metallic taste in my mouth that told me my system had been flooded with adrenaline.

A few moments later, Jaffar walked back into the room looking dishevelled. 'I'm sorry,' he said. 'Are you okay, Major Rabia?'

I was speechless. All I could think was, *Holy shit, what just happened?*

Then I turned around to see James looking similarly stunned. We stared at each other in absolute disbelief, each knowing what the other was thinking: *Did Jaffar just save our lives?* I quickly tried to process what had happened. There I was, a woman without a hijab – someone the police around me would have believed to be flouting their religion and their customs. They were Shiite Muslim extremists who believed in Sharia law, the same men behind a lot of the rapes and murders of liberal women in Basra. So I'd have presumed they would first and foremost have been angry with me, even before I'd tried bargaining with Judge Raghib in front of them. And yet ... I had the strongest, weirdest sense that Jaffar was trying to protect me.

Why? I couldn't help thinking it. If anything, Jaffar should have been pleased by the opportunity to get rid of James and me without having to do the dirty work himself. There was no doubt in my mind that he knew we were gathering intelligence on him, yet he made sure we stayed alive.

I looked at this man who'd just held my life in his hands and come down on the side of preserving it. I'd always dealt with him respectfully whenever I'd visited the Jamiat. I'd never let knowing what he was capable of affect my behaviour towards him. I'd dealt with him as one human being to another and perhaps that was what saved me – perhaps he respected me in turn.

I swallowed. There was an open window to my right, and through it I could hear people shouting – a rabble. I hadn't heard it the entire time the man with the gun was in the room, but at that moment I realised the noise was people in the compound screaming about what they should do to the foreigners.

Looking out the window, I saw an Iraqi with cameras trying to get through the crowd. He was being pushed and shoved in all directions and yet somehow he managed literally to crawl into the police station clutching his cameras. A minute or so later he entered the room where we were. He was a journalist. The police officers began insulting him. I couldn't help thinking, *The one thing that unites all of us in Basra is that we hate the bloody journalists*. James and I started giggling, and some of the others in the room had a chuckle as well.

Amid all this mayhem, four British soldiers from the same Special Forces unit as Ed and Di were pushed into the room with us. They'd tried to sneak into the compound and been caught, so now the police had six captives – plus Ed and Di, whose whereabouts we no longer knew. I was becoming increasingly anxious about where they might have been taken. The fact that there were now six of us being held was particularly ominous – just a year earlier, the same number of British Military Police officers had been held hostage and murdered in similar circumstances in a police station in another southern Iraq province.

Like James and me, the newcomers were allowed to keep their weapons – which I found more than odd, considering they were SAS. They were also allowed to keep the couple of two-way radios they had with them. This meant we had radio communication back to Special Forces, as well as back to our own brigade, and six guns between us. Still, we were by no means in control of the situation. The SCU police could have decided in an instant that they wanted us gone, and we would have been gone.

Before anything else, though, the SAS soldiers told us the violence outside the police station had got completely out of control. British tanks from the units trying to bring the chaos under control had been petrol-bombed, soldiers were on fire, and rocket-propelled grenades were going off everywhere. It had been obvious to us inside that things had become a lot worse because we could hear plenty of gunfire.

James and I brought the soldiers up to date on events inside the Jamiat – and the SAS team promptly announced they wanted to bust their way out of the room and try to rescue Ed and Di. They were hell-bent on what seemed to me an absolute suicide mission: guns blazing, shooting their way out of the room, then seeing if they could find their two colleagues. Special Forces are gods in the military; no one challenges them. James seemed to offer tacit agreement to their plan but I wasn't going to let their special status keep me quiet.

'You're joking, aren't you?' I said. 'Look around you! Look at the number of armed people in this room. You don't know where the guys are – you don't know whether they've been taken elsewhere.'

The soldiers stared at me, their faces impassive.

'We're all in this together,' I continued. 'One hundred per cent. You may be Special Forces, but I'm in this with you as well. It's my life you're gambling with, too, and I don't agree with your proposal because it will get us all killed. You're not going to rescue anybody. You need to focus on staying alive.' I looked at them. 'We need to keep together,' I added with emphasis.

A couple of them seemed to take my plea on board; they talked to the other two in low voices, thinking I couldn't hear them. 'She's got a point,' I heard one of them say.

In one sense I was surprised I'd had the gall to say anything at all. Without really thinking about it, I'd just lectured four of the most elite, highly trained and respected soldiers around. But I was so extremely fearful about any of us getting out of the police station alive that those were the thoughts uppermost in my mind.

The SAS soldiers stayed put, and several tense hours passed as the chaos continued outside the compound. During this time we remained standing at one end of the holding room while all the Iraqi men in the room continued to sneer and stare at us. As defiant as I felt, I couldn't ignore what they were doing. I could shut my eyes, but that would only have given them the satisfaction of knowing they'd affected me.

Finally we were all taken back to the DIA section of the Jamiat. On Jaffar's orders, his men formed a human shield to protect us as we were rushed through the SCU corridor, outside and into the neighbouring compound, leaving Jaffar behind us. As soon as we were in, the two-way radios began to crackle as the SAS men communicated with their command. James and I then borrowed the radios so we could talk to our own brigade headquarters. It was mildly reassuring to be able to talk to them – not only had it allowed us to give our colleagues an update on our situation, but the police hadn't tried to stop us talking, so they mustn't have been worried about us communicating with the army. Still, the atmosphere remained extremely tense.

Through the radio we heard that the brigadier and the British consul general were working on a diplomatic solution, trying to organise a letter from Basra's governor demanding everyone's release. Apparently they were also in negotiations with Baghdad, but it all seemed to be taking an awfully long time. I'd lost track of how many hours had passed since we arrived at al-Jamiat. All I knew was that I didn't want to spend as many hours again – or longer – waiting for the governor or someone in Baghdad to consent to our release. So I tried to reopen negotiations with Colonel Sewan, who, as the head of the DIA, was now the most senior officer present. My negotiations and meetings in the past had usually been with Colonel Sewan.

Through an interpreter I asked repeatedly to be able to go back and check on our two soldiers because I was worried about being separated from them. 'I demand to see our two soldiers,' I said finally. 'You must do this under the agreed law between our two nations. You must release them to me. You know you're breaking the law. You must at least let me see them, Colonel.'

But Colonel Sewan just kept saying, 'It's not in my hands.'

Then I twigged. 'Are our men still in the compound or have they been taken elsewhere?' I asked.

Sewan shrugged and replied, 'This is not under my control. I have no control of the situation.'

'You know me, you can trust me,' I told him. 'I'm a person of my word. I will do whatever is necessary to make sure they're brought to justice if they've done anything wrong. You must let me see them and talk to them again.'

'Major Rabia,' Colonel Sewan said abruptly in Arabic, 'there's no point.'

I understood this to mean that Ed and Di were gone – whether that meant removed from the Jamiat or killed, I couldn't tell.

Suddenly the atmosphere in the room shifted. About a third of the Shiite clerics we'd left behind in the SCU compound, when we moved back to the DIA, reappeared, in Colonel Sewan's office, along with some of the SCU police officers. Now they surrounded us.

By that stage we were all dehydrated and in desperate need of something to drink. Our captors gave us tap water, which usually we wouldn't have touched, but it was over fifty degrees, so we drank whatever we could. Perhaps their intention was to make us sick.

Then James and a couple of the SAS soldiers announced that they needed to relieve themselves. They were escorted outside by some of the police officers, who protected them from the angry crowd. By now the crowd had begun to disperse, but those remaining were still vocal and angry.

Through an interpreter, I said needed to go to the toilet as well and a number of the men in the room responded by laughing. They told me I could either go to the toilet right there in the room or go outside on my own. Outside – where the crowd was still baying for our blood, where rocket-propelled grenades and firebombs were going off everywhere. Outside – where what sounded like small bombs exploding were actually armoured vehicles and tanks bursting into flames. Outside – where British and US fast jets were flying over the compound. I wasn't about to risk my life by going outside alone, especially as I could tell how much it would amuse those men if I did just that. But nor was I going to pull my pants down in front of them.

So I peed in my pants. It was the lesser of all the evils. And we were sweating so profusely we were all wet through anyway. The clerics and policemen who were watching me closely and had guessed what I was doing thought it was hilarious. I could feel myself becoming angry. I wasn't upset; I didn't want to cry. What I felt was more like rage that I'd been placed in that position. But I'd done what I had to do to keep myself safe.

Finally, we got a radio call saying that a recovery operation was in progress. By that time it must have been about 7.30 pm. Despite this call, more time passed with no sign of the recovery operation. The idea of waiting any longer had become intolerable, so we negotiated an agreement of our own, in Colonel Sewan's presence, to allow us to leave. Colonel Sewan told us that he had no transport and we wouldn't risk walking the streets of the Hayaniyah district, so he agreed that we could leave the compound and it would be up to us to organise transport.

At about 9 pm the police who'd been detaining us – between thirty and forty of them – escorted us from the compound then raced to their vehicles. Within about ninety seconds they'd all scarpered. The crowd had pretty much gone as well. They would all have heard the fast jets and guessed it was time to get out. And by now we could hear many more tanks on their way. This was our recovery operation, finally about to start.

Despite the fact we'd negotiated our own release and four or five of our own tanks were now nearing the Jamiat, this was still an extremely dangerous situation. Our great fear was that part of the compound may have been booby-trapped. We debated what we should do – how we should get ourselves out of there – but, really, there was no choice. Somehow we had to get down to one corner of the compound, near the gates, so the soldiers in the tanks could see we were alive and well.

An order had obviously been given for one of the tanks to breach the wall rather than go in through the main entrance. To get to where the tanks could collect us, we had to wade through the sewers, open ditches built partly on the inside and partly on the outside of the compound. Our group was pulled into the second and third tanks, with James and me in the third. Ed and Di – our reason for being in the Jamiat in the first place – were in none of them.

Using video surveillance, one of our Sea King helicopters had spotted Ed and Di earlier, at around the time James, the four SAS soldiers and I were being hustled through to the DIA. Police had taken Ed and Di out of the compound and forced them into a car. The Sea King had then tracked the vehicle to a building we believed was perhaps a Hizbollah safe house. Our tanks now made a beeline for that house. The SAS soldiers manning the tanks conducted a search and fairly quickly brought out Ed and Di, who got in my tank.

Both were absolutely elated and told us how narrowly they'd just escaped execution. By the time the SAS soldiers arrived, the two had been wearing only their underwear – it's part of the ritual of beheading to be stripped of almost all your clothes before you're murdered. The men who'd been holding Ed and Di in the house and had since fled were either Hizbollah or Jaish al-Mahdi, they said. Ed, who was usually quite stoic, gave me the biggest hug. Di, a typical Welshman, gregarious and humorous, was swearing a great deal.

Once we were all safely inside the tank, Ed and Di started joking about the moment they first saw me back at the police station. To use their words, they'd thought they were 'truly fucked' when they realised that a woman – and a woman lawyer at that – had been sent in to save them.

We were all on an absolute high. It was a tremendous feeling, knowing every one of us had got through that horrendous experience with our lives. Very quickly, though, it was back to business, because we still had to travel in the tanks to our rendezvous point on the outskirts of the city. This was extremely risky because of who could have been after us, so during the twenty minutes it took to get to our rendezvous point we were all very tense.

At the rendezvous point we were picked up by choppers while the tanks made their way back to Shaibah Logistics Base. As I climbed into the helicopter bound for Basra Airport I felt utterly exhausted, but very relieved and ready for the remaining task at hand: the debrief. After every operation, I knew, there was a debrief, no matter how worn out anyone was.

A helicopter had brought me into this mess and now another was taking me away. That seemed about right, but it made it all seem a little surreal: *Did that really happen?*

Is this still the same chopper and I'm waiting to land? Did I just imagine it all?

I closed my eyes, thanked God for keeping me alive and prepared myself mentally for what I anticipated would be a long night back at base.

Chapter Thirteen

BETRAYAL

My memory of the helicopter flight back to base at Basra Airport is almost a complete blur. We were all lost in our own thoughts. James and I didn't talk in the chopper. The only thing he did say of a personal nature was when we were still in the back of the tank and he'd expressed huge relief that he would see his wife and young son again.

Once the chopper landed we all immediately headed for the SAS hangar. We were a big group. As well as the SAS guys, we were accompanied by some of the infantry and artillery soldiers who'd been involved in the recovery operation. A party atmosphere quickly developed. Ed and Di hugged me again, and several of their colleagues came up and said, 'Thanks for what you did.' There was a lot of mutual respect in that SAS hangar. People took photos, mainly of Ed and Di and me, and we all congratulated each other and expressed our relief that everyone had got back safely. Then we all left the SAS hangar and walked back through the doors into brigade headquarters.

James was immediately taken into the operations room, where I could see a big group of people waiting for him. I heard applause and saw someone – I think it was Rupert Jones, our chief of staff – shaking his hand. Then Brigadier John Lorimer did the same. But rather than be asked to follow James into the operations room, I was led down the corridor to my office, where a group of my female colleagues and the padre were waiting with a plate of biscuits and sand-wiches. I was given a cup of tea, and there were chitchat and pleasantries – 'Thank goodness you're fine', that sort of thing. I was bewildered – I was fairly sure James was being debriefed in that operations room, but no one seemed ready to debrief me. Tea and chat did not a debrief make.

A short time later, Brigadier Lorimer came in, gave me a hug and told me how relieved he was that I'd made it back safely. There had been some hairy moments, he said. I couldn't have agreed more. 'Well done! Well done!' he said. And then he suggested I go off and have 'a good rest'.

'Brigadier, I'm fine,' I replied. 'Don't I need to be debriefed? There's so much information I need to give you. I'm quite happy to be debriefed while everything is fresh in my mind.'

'No, that's fine,' he said. 'We'll talk later. Get some rest.' Then he suggested to a couple of my female colleagues that they take me back to my portacabin.

Being told to go and rest was the last thing I'd expected. I'd prepared myself for a few hours of debriefing at least. As I understood it, it was standard procedure, and I couldn't understand why standard procedure wouldn't be followed in this case.

The brigadier's approach also seemed to me, psychologically, to be the worst he could have taken. I was well aware of correct post-operational procedures. The last thing anyone should do when someone comes out of a conflict situation, such as the one we'd just been through at al-Jamiat, is give them a pat on the head and an exhortation to rest. On the contrary, there'd usually be a period of celebration and camaraderie before the returnees or survivors were asked to talk and 'download' while they were watched for signs of trauma. It seemed no one was planning to watch out for signs of trauma in me. *What's going on here?* I wondered.

Despite the brigadier's desire for me to rest, my adrenaline levels were sky high and my heart was still thumping. I'd gone through the mental process of organising, in chronological order, everything I needed to tell the brigadier, Rupert and anyone else. There was so much intelligence to pass on – or so I'd thought.

I realised the brigadier's behaviour had been paternal – he'd gone from being my commander to acting as a type of father figure. While I understood this – and was appreciative of some of that sentiment – it made me uncomfortable as well. If he'd just given me a hug as a completely spontaneous expression of emotion, then said something like, 'Right, have your cup of tea and then will you be okay to debrief?' I'd have appreciated this unconditionally, because the paternal approach would have been combined with professionalism. His approach, however, seemed more primary school than professional to me. And I still had no idea why I wasn't being debriefed as James was. Whatever the reason, I definitely feel it was a poor judgement on Brigadier Lorimer's part.

To be fair to him, I wasn't a pretty sight. I stank of all sorts of things, including the sewers, and I was wet to the bone. But James was in exactly the same state, and had been judged fit to be shaken by the hand and patted on the back.

And so my female colleagues took me back to my accommodation at Waterloo Lines and we chatted for a while about trivial things, like the fact that my boots were ruined. They also described some of the reports they'd heard coming through about the violence taking place outside al-Jamiat, and how worried they'd been for me. Eventually I went off for a shower and when I came back they'd gone.

Sleep was impossible that night. Adrenaline was still racing through me. I was agitated and alone; there was so much going on in my head. Increasingly I was thinking, *This isn't right.* The right thing to do was debrief me. The right thing to do was get the whole story from *all* of the people who were there. My sense of right and wrong – always firm – was now heightened, and not just on my own behalf. I was interested in the truth. If they weren't debriefing me and getting my side of the story, they weren't interested in the truth. They just wanted one version. And I knew that one version wasn't enough.

After two or three hours I began getting stomach cramps and shortly afterwards became very ill, no doubt from the water we'd been given all those hours earlier at the police station. For the next twelve hours or so I had diarrhoea and vomiting. There wasn't a hell of a lot I could do about this, which was also frustrating, because I knew there was going to be a meeting the following morning about the entire Jamiat affair. I sent a message asking if the meeting could be delayed until I was able to crawl in at some point in the afternoon, but I didn't hear back.

The brigadier wasn't in his office when I dropped around to visit. I remember asking someone whether I was needed for a debrief.

'No,' came the answer. They had all the information they needed.

By this stage, the Jamiat incident had gone on to become a big international story and a headache for the Blair government because it finally exposed the reality of the precarious security situation with the Basra police. In Downing Street the political fallout was quite severe, particularly given that the initial reaction to the incident by the Basra Governorate and the Iraqi Government was temporarily to withdraw cooperation with allied forces in southern Iraq.

The Basra governor issued a statement the day after the incident, which said the 'attack' on the Iraqi Police Service compound by British forces was a demonstration of the lack of respect we had for their authority and the sanctity of the Iraqi rule of law. I of course found this particularly infuriating, given all the work we'd done with the Iraqi judicial authorities to help them re-establish the rule of law in their region – to say nothing of their constant requests for us to clean up and get rid of the Jamiat police station once and for all.

The governor of Basra and the Iraqi Government both denied any knowledge of or involvement in the events at the Jamiat, despite the fact that on the day we were in al-Jamiat Brigadier Lorimer and the British consul general had managed to obtain a letter from Basra's governor confirming that Ed and Di were members of the British Armed Forces. That letter had been delivered to al-Jamiat by Lieutenant Colonel Nick Henderson, commander of the Coldstream Guards. So while the governor might deny that anything had taken place, there was hard evidence that something had.

Still, the governor and the Iraqi Government denounced the British military, giving news and media statements to the effect that the army's actions were totally reprehensible and inexcusable, and making it clear they would no longer cooperate with the British. So it was likely that the brigadier was out trying to mend some fences that day.

My brigade colleagues seemed unable to talk to me about what had happened, talking to me about everything *except* the Jamiat affair. I on the other hand wanted to talk about it, but whenever I raised the matter, it seemed to make them uncomfortable and they would change the subject. It felt like a wall of silence had gone up around me.

Padre Maynard came to see me and said he hadn't known where to put himself when the brigadier hugged me and sent me off to bed, describing his actions as both sexist and patronising. The padre had worked with Special Forces and the elite Parachute Regiment in the past. He'd seen and heard a great deal over the years and was battle-hardened. That he mentioned the brigadier's behaviour seemed to me to say it had stood out to him as unusual.

In thinking about the reasons why my role in what happened at the Jamiat was covered up, one possibility that occurred to me was that Rupert Jones had countermanded the brigadier by ordering me to go into the Jamiat. Maybe it became necessary to keep this quiet because of the political ramifications of a foreign, female, Muslim lawyer being sent in to negotiate the release of two SAS soldiers. I wasn't just a soldier acting for other soldiers – I was a lawyer. This wasn't how the situation would usually have played out, and that would have been embarrassing for the army, and for the government.

The flap over the media reports coming out in Iraq and in Britain caused some panic at our base. All the senior officers were working flat out to restore diplomatic relations. The problem was that, at home, the British public was once again asking all the old questions about Iraq: Why had we gone there? What were we still doing there? What good were we doing?

Everything that various political and military figures had tried so hard to keep a lid on – including the rotten state of the Iraqi Police Service – was now exploding in the media, although so far I'd had no contact with the media myself. My colleagues back home had obviously been talking about what had happened, because the director of my corps, Major General David Howell, telephoned and later wrote to me in Iraq to see if I was all right. He was an affable man and I appreciated the call.

When I asked General Howell if there'd been any media inquiries, he said he was glad I'd raised the subject, because one of the things he'd wanted to check with me was whether it was okay to say I'd been involved in the Jamiat incident if journalists did contact him. He was keen to publicise the sterling job one of his officers had done – and in particularly trying circumstances, he added.

'Thank you, Sir, but can I think about whether I'm happy for you to give my name? I haven't had the opportunity to speak to my husband yet,' I replied.

He offered to contact Anthony on my behalf but I said I'd prefer to do that myself. I knew that if the first Anthony heard about the Jamiat affair was from the major general and not me, he'd be extremely concerned. He was, of course, the first person I'd wanted to speak to, and the only reason I hadn't spoken to him straight away was that I was still awaiting permission. By great good fortune a very dear friend of ours who was on duty at the Permanent Joint Headquarters in London while the Jamiat events were unfolding was able to tell Anthony I was all right.

David Howell told me to stay in touch and let him know whether he could help in any way by speaking to my family. He was very obliging and very concerned. 'The whole corps is so proud of you,' he added. 'We can't wait till you get back.'

Ed and Di were forced to leave Basra, since it was impossible for them to remain after what had happened, so I didn't see them again, but their colleagues in the SAS came to see me on a number of occasions in those days after Jamiat. One of the men who'd been taken hostage with us came several times. I knew he was checking on me to make sure I was okay, and I appreciated it.

There were policies and standard operating procedures in place when it came to mental health care and post-operational care of armed forces personnel. Commanding and senior officers had a duty of care to observe and monitor their staff and refer staff for counselling or therapy where there were any concerns regarding their emotional or mental wellbeing. There was also an expectation that commanding officers would know each and every member of their unit and would informally interact with them so that they were approachable if their men or women had problems or concerns that needed to be discussed. A commanding officer was expected to be able to detect when something was 'not right' and take appropriate action to get the right care for his soldiers.

There were also very clear policies with regards to post-operational care of soldiers and officers. All those who served in Iraq were entitled to post-operational leave, but before taking that leave people had to go through a period (at least a few days) of what was called 'decompression' in a neutral place (often Cyprus), away from the theatre of war – but also away from families. Normalisation, debriefing and de-stressing were meant to take place during this decompression period, as well as formal and informal mental and emotional preparation for returning home and the challenges that would present.

The reality was that some units and commanding officers were better at managing this care than others. This pastoral care aspect of service was almost always left to the discretion of the senior and commanding officers.

As a legal officer who was only attached to the brigade for the period of the deployment to Iraq, my assessment was that I wasn't really seen as a permanent fixture of the brigade and one that the brigadier felt he had complete responsibility for, despite what I had been through and the work I had done.

I think I fell between the cracks – the brigade assumed I would be supported by my Legal Corps and vice versa. The upshot was that I received no decompression and was told I wasn't eligible for it, and no one was looking out for signs of distress or trauma in my case.

I felt that I had to maintain a stiff upper lip. Stupidly, I thought that if I showed emotion, particularly as a female officer, it would be interpreted as weakness and a vulnerability I didn't want anyone in the army to see at that point.

I believe now, with all the cases and publicity surrounding PTSD, the forces have been compelled to give more attention and importance to mental health care for their soldiers. I am not certain but I suspect that some post-operational counselling or therapy is now mandatory, not discretionary, and doesn't rely on self-referral, so I think over time lessons in this regard have been learnt.

Lieutenant Colonel Alex Taylor, a legal officer attached to the Multi National Division next door, was also a great comfort. Concerned that I hadn't been debriefed, I went to see him and told him everything that had occurred, both before and after I'd returned from the Jamiat. Being debriefed is standard military procedure and I could not understand why it had not been followed in my case. To me it symbolised the army's belief that I had nothing to say that they wanted to hear – and for that reason I was sidelined and ignored. I saw it also as a missed opportunity for them, as I had a lot of intelligence to pass on. I had been the only one from our side who spoke

Arabic. There were things I had learnt during the incident at the Jamiat that would have been useful.

I went on to tell Alex I was extremely upset that I hadn't been able to tell my side of the story and felt no one was willing to listen to me. As I spoke I could feel myself becoming steadily angrier.

Alex was shocked and worried. He asked if I'd like him to speak to the brigadier but I said I thought it might only make things worse and it was best if I spoke to him myself first.

'Well, something must be done,' he replied.

I offered Alex my theory that perhaps in sending me into the Jamiat Rupert Jones had disobeyed the brigadier and that perhaps Rupert wanted to distance himself from the incident if he could. Alex agreed this was possible and was surprised Rupert had ordered me to go. But it was only a theory running around in my head along with my nagging doubt, my distress and the seeming silence from those around me. I felt, once more, a stranger in a strange land – except this time I had no idea why.

Eventually we agreed that he would hold off doing anything until I'd had a chance to talk to Brigadier Lorimer myself. If I didn't manage to, then Alex – as a more senior legal officer, even though he wasn't attached to my chain of command – would have a word with him. I managed to get some time with the brigadier the following day, but by that time Alex had already spoken to him on my behalf.

The brigadier didn't waste time. 'I understand you have concerns,' he said immediately.

'Yes, Sir,' I replied.

Before I managed to get another word out, the brigadier told me that if I felt my position was untenable, he was quite happy to give me permission to go back to the UK right away. I thought Brigadier Lorimer looked steely as he made this suggestion, and slightly uncomfortable, too. But he also seemed to think we had nothing more to discuss.

His suggestion alarmed me. Why would my position be untenable? Why should I go back to the UK? Surely I'd done nothing wrong? Before the end of my tour I wanted to be sure that the human rights work I was doing was going to achieve the right results. Leaving wasn't an option. So my response was equally swift: 'No, Sir,' I told him, 'I'm not going to go home. I've come here to do a job, I have a duty, and with your permission I'd like to soldier on until the end of my tour.'

'Yes, that's fine,' he answered.

*

With the events of the Jamiat still swirling around me I simply got back to work. There was no point sitting around waiting for things to change or wallowing in what couldn't be changed. There was too much else to do.

Within a fortnight the armed forces managed to mend bridges with the Basra Government, and operations in response to the Jamiat incident began as the army attempted to regain control of the area. As the army embarked on sweeps across Basra, I was called on to perform the traditional role of a military lawyer for the first time during my tour: I had to give advice on which targets were genuine and lawful, and which weren't. I also had to advise on search, arrest and detention procedures, and on the rules of engagement.

Most of those detained by the army were Iraqi Police Service officers whom we knew were Jaish al-Mahdi. They'd been arrested from different places – either from their homes or from the meeting places where they'd been planning their next operation. I was never present when they were picked up, but when they were brought in I was always at Shaibah Logistics Base, where the interrogations took place.

The reaction when these men saw me was mixed. Some of the prisoners – those who recognised me – hurled abuse: 'You call yourself a Muslim? You're a traitor!' Most, however, took a different, if probably predictable line: 'Major Rabia, we're innocent. Can you see what they're doing? This is so unfair. Help us. Explain to them that we helped you. We have a good relationship with you. We're police.'

None of them were forthcoming when they were inter-rogated. They were all very well trained, very loyal to Jaish al-Mahdi. It didn't matter what questions they were asked; they simply kept repeating, 'You've got the wrong person. We're innocent. We're police officers.'

My job at Shaibah Logistics Base was to monitor the con-ditions in which the detainees were kept and, of course, to watch the interrogations. This was the stuff I'd been trained to do – and which I would have been doing day in, day out had I been sent to Iraq in 2003, the year of the invasion. But it was still confronting. I discovered that dealing with real interrogations required a different kind of strength and control. In fact, there came a point during this period when I felt troubled and tense, simply because my role now was the polar opposite of how I'd spent the rest of my tour.

I'd taken a lot of pleasure in the fact that the sort of work I'd been involved in before had been far removed from such standard military activity as detention and interrogations. I certainly didn't feel like a traitor when the Jaish al-Mahdi insurgents were brought in for questioning, though. I played my role as a military lawyer willingly. Just because I had a Muslim background didn't mean I wasn't interested in upholding the rule of law, and I wasn't going to listen to anyone who tried to tell me otherwise.

All the same, I felt real sadness and frustration that all the good work the British had done in an attempt to restore justice in southern Iraq seemed to have been in vain. This feeling hit me when I was at Shaibah one day, watching a group of detainees being ushered off the back of a Land Rover. They were blindfolded and had plasticuffs around their hands, which was entirely legal and justifiable as we couldn't have them knowing where we were taking them. As I witnessed this scene, I thought, *Yes, this is absolutely what we should be doing, weeding out these insurgents and terrorists who've infiltrated the police.*

My brain had no trouble reasoning that we needed to do this and, in fact, I thought we should have been doing it months earlier, as the Baswaris had been constantly asking us to. But as a human being, I did have to wrestle with such a confronting scenario. I think anyone would have. Islam – as my cultural background, as the religion I was now learning more about – didn't come into these feelings. I regarded the men we'd arrested as murderers and criminals who were misusing and abusing their position to justify their actions in the name of Islam.

As well – and in my view this is just as significant – I can't think of a single incident during the interrogations when I had to step in and remind our men of their obligations. I never had to say 'You're not doing this lawfully' or 'You shouldn't be doing that'.

Like everyone else, I'm aware that questions had been raised in the years beforehand, after the invasion of Iraq, concerning the treatment of Iraqis who'd been detained by the British in Basra. But in 2005, when I was in Iraq, in the operations I witnessed and was involved in for a few weeks that September and October, I can say hand on heart that the conduct of the soldiers was completely professional. I witnessed no rough treatment whatsoever. There was no breach of international conventions or international law – I'd have been onto it instantly if there had been. My colleagues also knew I would insist on being present for every interrogation and would resist being 'managed' in any way so that they could act illegally.

Every interrogation I saw was conducted in a professional, measured, appropriate and controlled manner. The way the soldiers operated during the operations I saw was equally professional and restrained. That's one thing I must stress, and it's to the British Army's absolute credit. Its soldiers were potentially arresting and detaining people they knew had been responsible for the deaths of some of their own colleagues. I could almost have understood if they'd needed restraining or reminding about their responsibilities as they carried out their sweeps. But they were just outstanding – at least at this end of the country.

These operations in Basra went on for two or three weeks, which probably doesn't seem like a very long time but it was an incredibly intense period. I was working 24-hour shifts, and sometimes 32-hour shifts if operations were unfolding – not to mention the hours and hours of planning that went into them. It was also the work I'd gone there to do – the work I'd joined the army to do – to help make Basra, and Iraq, safer for its people.

It was my old passion – giving a voice to the powerless – that motivated me, both to go there in the first place and then to continue working so hard when I was there. Of course, in ensuring the human rights of the people we arrested, some people would argue that I was helping the powerful against the powerless, but that's not how I see it. In a perfect world these people would never have done the things they'd done and we wouldn't have had to arrest them. But they did. As a lawyer charged with ensuring that the legal safeguards created to protect human rights were being put into place, it was my job to do everything I could to restore that protection to the lives of *all* Iraqis. Removing these men from the streets of Basra was an important part of that.

What had happened at the Jamiat – what happened after, in my own workplace – did not make me vengeful. I did not want to put all these men in jail because they reminded me of the men who'd restrained my liberty and attempted to take away my dignity. I was doing my job. It was hard work. It was tiring work. But it was work worth doing. And however tired I felt, however hard it was, I was always aware that the people of Basra had been doing it far tougher for a very long time.

CHAPTER FOURTEEN

INQUIRIES AND TRAGEDIES

Word came through that the Iraqi authorities wanted an inquiry into the Jamiat incident. That was one of their conditions before they agreed to start cooperating in a small way with the British again. The British agreed to do this, although I think it was viewed on our side solely as a political and public relations exercise to help us restore normal relations with the Iraqi Government and regain their cooperation.

It was Alex Taylor who told me there was to be an inquiry. He knew what was going on politically and strategically with the foreign forces in Iraq because of his position as legal officer in the Multi National Division. Alex told me the British Government had appointed a retired brigadier to come over to Iraq and do some fact-finding, and to question people from both the British and Iraqi sides.

Although I made it clear I was keen to be involved in the inquiry, I wasn't called upon to give evidence. Brigadier

Lorimer told me I wasn't required. He said I was too busy, they had all the information they needed and James could tell them anything else they needed to know.

'All right, Brigadier, if that's the decision, then that's the decision,' I replied at the time, but only because I suspected that becoming angry would harm my position. In reality, I was furious. At this point I did wonder, *What am I doing here?* The thought of going back to London had crossed my mind, but apart from that being exactly what Brigadier Lorimer had suggested I do, I was really hoping the security situation would improve and I'd be able to resume some of my human rights duties before I left Basra. Unfortunately, the bad atmosphere in Basra after the Jamiat incident had made it too dangerous for any of us to leave base.

I desperately wanted to visit some of the Iraqis I hadn't seen for a while and talk to them face to face. I wanted to explain that I hadn't forsaken them or forgotten them. I wanted them to hear what had happened at the Jamiat from me – because I knew stories would have been told about the 'Israeli spies' and the people sent in to rescue them, including the easily identifiable female lawyer with the Arabic name. I didn't want the Iraqis I knew to think I'd been lying to them about who I was and the work I did.

So I learnt very little about the British inquiry, except for the fact that it didn't hear my version of events. I did hear that a journalist from Al Jazeera turned up at the gates of our headquarters asking to speak with me at one point, as did some local journalists, but apparently they were all turned away, which was the general policy at the base.

This was a standard response unless the military wanted to make media statements of their own or the British Government agreed to certain interviews. No one from the British media got in touch, although Major General David Howell did tell me later that the ALS had been contacted by journalists wanting to know what my role in the Jamiat incident had been. I found out afterwards that the corps had been directed to give a 'no comment' response. This was a clear change from the director's initial desire to promote his officer publicly.

I'd emailed the general not long after we'd spoken on the phone, confirming that I was now happy for my name to be released, if he thought that was appropriate.

James Woodham was called upon to give evidence at the British inquiry, as were some of the SAS soldiers and some of the key commanders of the forces outside the Jamiat – those, particularly the Coldstream Guards, who'd tried to hold back the crowd. The officers involved in the recovery operation were also invited to give evidence, as were more senior figures such as the brigadier, who'd been working at a diplomatic level post-Jamiat to restore relations with the Iraqis. It seemed to me I was the only one involved who wasn't invited to give evidence. You may well ask how any of these men, and especially James Woodham, could describe the events at the Jamiat without mentioning my role. I have no idea what any of them said, because as I hadn't been invited to appear at the inquiry, no one would discuss it with me – that appeared to be the protocol. I had some good contacts in divisional intelligence and they kept me informed about who was giving evidence from the British and Iraqi sides. But that was all the information I received.

Another level to my outrage at my exclusion was the blatant gender inequality. While my information would be valuable to the investigation, more to the point, I felt I'd been side-lined because in the army's eyes my view as a woman wasn't as important as all the men's views. Basically they thought that there was nothing I could add that a man couldn't say for me.

People often talk about having a 'gut feeling' for things; sometimes it feels like a curdling, which is the sense that something is wrong; sometimes it is a swirling cauldron, which is fear and anger all at once. Each time I thought about the inquiry or heard a piece of information about what was taking place there, I experienced one of these states. I knew it all felt wrong: if they didn't have me there, how could they get at the truth?

Far more powerful than my sense of indignation at not being included was the gnawing feeling in my belly that this army I'd sworn to serve, that I'd risked my life to serve, was not interested in the real truth, just a certain version of it. Some of us had risked our lives to go after the men we'd just detained in the sweeps. We were risking our lives just by staying in Basra. And for what? *What are we doing here?* I thought.

Even when I was a very little girl, I'd always demanded the truth. This hadn't always made for a comfortable life and was probably a factor in the difficulty between my parents and me. Now, in a foreign land, far away from the husband I loved, I felt as if my work with the army was built on lies. And that disgusted me.

Part of the agreement between the Iraqis and the Brits was that the British Government would release a draft report from its own inquiry in very short order, so the Iraqis could look at it before it was released. I understand, however, that the Iraqis weren't at all happy with what they read. They felt that the brigadier tasked with leading the inquiry had glossed over some key points surrounding the Jamiat incident, including the events beforehand that had led to the two SAS soldiers being detained that would not have painted the British Government and the military in a good light.

Neither Ed nor Di had been doing anything unusual or different when they went off on a covert operation to gather intelligence about Jaffar's movements. The problem had been more to do with them operating during a period of very high sensitivity because of Ahmed al-Fartusi's arrest only a couple of days earlier. I'm aware that rumours started circulating later on about explosives allegedly being found in their car by Iraqi police, but I'd be very surprised if that were the case. The operation Ed and Di were conducting at the time was focused on surveillance, and there was no intention for them to engage in any combat. They had opened fire when trapped by the road block, which was standard procedure to avoid compromising their mission and identity. It would have been highly unlikely that they were shooting to kill just to make a getaway in their vehicle.

When the Iraqis decided to launch an inquiry of their own, to be headed by Iraq's minister of the Interior, Baqir Solagh Jabr, they made it very clear to the British Government and Brigadier Lorimer that they wanted to hear from

Major Rabia. They knew I hadn't given evidence at our own inquiry, and they considered this another key omission. The British agreed to let me appear at the Iraqi inquiry, although I believe they did so reluctantly, knowing that if they didn't the Iraqis would see it as an attempt at a cover-up. It would also have made them appear uncooperative – and by this stage the relationship between the British and the Iraqis was hanging on by its fingernails. The British Government was desperately concerned to restore goodwill with the Iraqi Government because all the publicity was harming Tony Blair.

I don't think my own side realised the Iraqis were fully aware of my involvement in the events at al-Jamiat. I think they also underestimated the information the Iraqis had about me, and how well known I was, even up in Baghdad. The old-school former brigadier who'd come over on behalf of the British Government to run the British inquiry seemed to me to think a woman's story wasn't as important as a man's – there was no point having me at the inquiry because James could speak for me. Perhaps the army thought the Iraqis would care as little about me and my involvement as they did, and for similar reasons.

I keep finding myself coming back to the interpretation that the main reason – perhaps the only reason – I wasn't included in the British inquiry and hadn't been given the opportunity to tell my story about Jamiat was that I was a woman. I've struggled to understand why my sex has anything to do with anything. Maybe, because I hadn't kowtowed to the authority of the men present that day, I was now being put in my place. Or maybe they just didn't know what to do with me. There was no precedent for this – never before had a female army lawyer been held for hours by antagonistic forces in a foreign land. So in an organisation that thrived on rules, on doing things the way they'd always been done, there was nowhere to fit me. And so, it seemed to me, it was easier just to pretend I didn't exist.

In due course, the Iraqi Minister of the Interior and his cabinet arrived in Basra and the Iraqi inquiry opened. I went along to Basra Palace, where the inquiry was being held, accompanied by James Woodham, Brigadier Lorimer and a couple of commanding officers. We'd had briefings beforehand about the 'line' we were to take; I was very aware that the directions about what we could and couldn't say had come from London. Essentially, I was told to say I was sent in after James to assist with negotiations because I'd been asked for by Judge Raghib. I was not asked to lie – just to keep the story brief and consistent with stories told by the others.

Rather than being called in one by one to give evidence, we all sat in a large room like a boardroom, with the Iraqis on one side of a long table and the British on the other. Brigadier Lorimer had insisted we all give our evidence in front of each other. In particular, my colleagues wanted me to explain to the Iraqis that under the Status of Forces Agreement the police should have handed over Ed and Di as soon as they'd identified themselves as British military personnel. Even though I'd mentioned to my colleagues my feelings of being sidelined and ignored, it seemed not to occur to any of my colleagues that this was my first opportunity to have some sort of debriefing, albeit weeks after the Jamiat incident – and it was all thanks to the Iraqis. Still, I had no intention of breaking ranks and saying anything unscripted, no matter how much it galled me not to. I was determined to be professional.

The Iraqis regarded our side of the table quite coldly. They made it clear they weren't at all happy with the British investigation, which made the dynamics very unsettling. When the Iraqis asked why I hadn't given evidence at the British inquiry given the key role I'd played in the Jamiat incident, the brigadier said I'd been ill then added that I'd also been very busy. James had given evidence for both of us, the brigadier went on, because he'd been at al-Jamiat from the start and they hadn't wanted to put me through another ordeal. It was a patronising response in my view.

One of the Iraqi officials looked at me at this point. I just smiled. The Iraqis didn't pursue it any further, but I don't think it was because they didn't want to know more. They knew me by now and I'd come to know them, so I believe they stopped that line of inquiry because they knew the predicament it would have put me in.

The last day of the Iraqi inquiry was exhausting. It was also emotionally draining and frustrating because I'd felt constrained the entire time I was there. There was so much more I could have said – and I think the Iraqis suspected this, too. It was nightfall when we finally left Basra Palace. In the Middle East, in desert areas like Basra, it goes literally pitch black when night falls, and we had a general policy not to travel at nightfall because it was so dangerous.

The rule obviously had to be ignored on this occasion, though. We had a ten-minute walk to the helicopter that was taking us back to base, with soldiers all around us. As we were crossing the helicopter landing zone, a young soldier in front of me suddenly tripped and landed face down, hard on the ground. He tripped over so quickly that I fell over him and straight onto one of the large rusty metal brackets used to tie down helicopters in high winds. The bracket went right through my knee, all the way to the bone. I was in excruciating pain and couldn't move. A special medical helicopter had to be organised to take me to our field hospital at Shaibah. As the others went off in the first helicopter back to brigade headquarters, I couldn't help thinking that once again I was on my own, through circumstances beyond my control.

I'd injured my knee so badly it needed surgery, so I spent the next few days in hospital, where I reached a very low point and questioned in earnest why I was there. September had really been a horror month. Just before the Jamiat incident, we'd lost one of our senior intelligence officers, Major Matt Bacon, when he was killed by a roadside bomb. Two of our soldiers, Stephen Manning and Donal Meade, had been killed by another bomb only a few days earlier. I couldn't help thinking that everything seemed to be going from bad to worse.

Desperate to leave hospital and get back to work, I pretty much got the staff to discharge me the moment I was able to manage my military-issue crutches. The security situation was still bad, so I had to get back to base by chopper. I hobbled onto the helicopter landing zone still feeling

181

depressed – and who should be waiting there but Captain Ken Masters, the commanding officer of the British Royal Military Police's Special Investigations Branch?

The majority of the military police weren't held in great affection by members of the army because of the job they did, but I'd come across Ken before and we got along very well. We had a chat while we were waiting for our transport, and I told him fragments of the Jamiat story. We spent much longer talking about his family, though, because Ken's tour was ending in about a week and he was returning to the UK.

It was lovely to have that human contact and speak to someone freely about the incident. Ken and I kept talking on the flight back. He didn't reveal much more about himself during that conversation. He said only that it had been a very difficult tour and he'd been fighting his own demons. He was very relieved it was coming to an end, he repeated, because he couldn't wait to get home and see his wife and daughters.

A couple of nights later I saw Ken again. There was a room at Waterloo Lines with a TV and a fridge, where the officers could go and chill out when not on duty. Ken was sitting on the sofa in the darkness, watching TV. We had another quick chat and then I went off to my portacabin to bed.

The next day, Ken took his own life.

It was the afternoon when I heard the terrible news that he'd hanged himself in his portacabin. Ken's death was inves-tigated by some people from his own regiment of the Royal Military Police, and within a very short time I found myself giving evidence of a very different nature, after it turned out I'd been the last person to speak to him. During the awful period after Ken's death I spent weeks beating myself up. I was furious with myself for being so preoccupied with what I was going through with my knee and the inquiries when it was clear, looking back, that Ken hadn't been himself.

He'd been sitting in the dark, watching TV. That wasn't normal. If I'd spent a few minutes with him, and asked him why he was sitting in the dark by himself, might he have opened up? Maybe that was all he needed just to last the three more days before he went home to be with his family. I felt incredibly selfish and kept asking myself whether, had I done things differently, Ken would still be alive. It was a normal reaction, I suppose, to an abnormal situation.

Ken's suicide made me realise how precious and fragile life is – and how, in Iraq, we were all living in such a pressure-cooker environment and in such an unusual state physically, emotionally and mentally. Ken's death also served as a stark example to me of what could happen when someone wasn't treated well. All sorts of questions were raised after Ken's death about whether he was being bullied or had received adequate support from his superiors, which was something he alluded to in his suicide note. It was a classic example of how badly the military managed its people, and how little attention it paid to the mental health needs of its soldiers and officers – particularly in situations of high pressure.

Inevitably, it also made me very aware that Ken's fate could potentially have been mine. There was no doubt that I was in a fragile state at the time. The only thing that saved me, really, was the resilience I'd first learnt in childhood and had rediscovered in the years since. In Iraq I prayed more than

I ever had in my life. It wasn't about Islam or Christianity. I was constantly praying for strength and wisdom, resilience and guidance. I prayed pretty much during my whole time in Iraq, especially when I realised I'd taken on this incredible responsibility for others – namely the Iraqis I was trying to help. And I kept praying after the Jamiat incident when I felt I no longer had control over my actions or my future.

When the security situation deteriorated and every week in the latter half of the tour someone was killed, I prayed I wouldn't be killed by a bomb that day, as so many others had been. I prayed that I'd live to see another day. I prayed to God for strength and guidance – but I also asked Him why, when I'd always acted with the best of intentions, I wasn't being treated with more respect. Towards the end of my tour, though, I was simply saying, 'Well, okay, I don't know why and I'll probably never know why, but just give me the strength to see this through and maybe one day I'll understand.'

The sum of our life's experiences keeps accumulating as we grow older. I'd had difficulties – at the age of nine, after I left school and most recently at the Jamiat. Individually, the parts of my life that had been difficult could have broken me. Situations like that have broken others. Taken together, though – and given that I survived them – they made me stronger. With each bad situation, I'd learnt more about my capacity not only to take care of myself but to be true to myself. I was strong. I was resilient. And had it not been for that I could easily have ended up like Ken. No one apart from the padre and Alex Taylor seemed to think that the army's approach with me after Jamiat might have an adverse effect. Nor did they think about the effect Ken's suicide might have had on me, on top of everything else.

The padre organised a memorial service for Ken before his body was taken back to the UK. In the weeks afterwards, I often thought about his wife and daughters, waiting there for his body to be returned to them. I know there were a lot of questions about Ken's death, and about his commanding officer – and also the treatment of other military police officers who'd performed similar roles. A lot of information about these issues was 'managed', shall we say? I saw a very ugly side to the British forces during that period.

In light of Ken's death the army could have – should have – reviewed their policies about mental health. I do not know if they did anything then, but mental health support was certainly reviewed once the link between PTSD and suicides became very public between 2007 and 2009.

The Iraqis duly released their report to the Iraqi prime minister, Nouri al-Maliki. The British Government received a copy later on. The Basra governor used excerpts from the report for his own requirements. Diplomatic agreements were then put in place to make sure certain things were attended do – such as repairing the al-Jamiat police station – before full cooperation with allied forces was restored in the south. And that was that. I don't remember any huge political fallout caused by the Iraqi inquiry, and very slowly full cooperation between the Iraqis and the British resumed.

I asked my own chain of command on several occasions for a copy of the Iraqi report, but was never given one, although I did hear from Iraqi contacts that I was mentioned in it, along with the work I'd been doing, including my human rights work with Sunni torture victims and families of those who'd disappeared. As would be expected when a large document is cut down to a very short one, the summary of the report's conclusions released to the media made no mention of me.

The one steadfast aspect of my story is that I never breached protocol or security, or leaked information – even though it would have been very, very easy to do so, given my contacts and the fact that the reporter's mobile phone footage taken of me in front of and inside al-Jamiat was still doing the rounds of insurgents and locals. I remained professional – and loyal to the army – to the end.

CHAPTER FIFTEEN

COMING HOME

My tour of duty in Basra ended a few weeks after Ken Masters' death, in November.

There was no farewell party of any kind because everyone in the brigade was returning to Britain and a brigade based in Germany was replacing us. We all carried on working damn hard until the very last minute, then jumped on the plane and flew back to the UK.

I was one of the very last to return. Before I left Basra, I attended a last round of meetings with the Sunni clerics and Chief Judge Laith, but since I was with Brigadier Lorimer, I didn't feel I could speak to them openly. I simply thanked them and expressed my regret that I couldn't have done more while I was there. I was sad that I didn't get the chance to have the conversations I wanted to have with these men who'd placed such trust in me.

I wanted to explain to them that the Jamiat incident and what followed were not my fault or my doing; to tell them that I was not allowed to continue with my work with them, despite my strong wishes. I also wanted to find out if I could do anything from the UK to assist them in the work that they would continue to do in my absence. But I would never have the chance to say any of it.

The chief judge took my hand and placed his on top. 'Thank you for what you've done,' he said. 'I know you've really tried to make a difference.' Then he turned to the brigadier and added, 'There's a lot more work to be done.'

Although I was leaving behind that work, I did feel we'd accomplished some good things while I was there. One project I'd been able to organise early in my tour, during a trip Chris Hughes and I made to Baghdad, was getting an agreement from the chief justice of Iraq to put a working group together with the aim of setting up an Iraqi Complaints Commission. This commission would consist of a board of retired judges who would hear and investigate complaints of police corruption. I know the chief justice agreed to this in principle, and a very similar body was formed the following year.

And there were some upbeat moments before I left Basra, in particular when I went to see the vehicles for the new Basra Prison Escort Service and met the officers who'd been recruited.

Most importantly, I was able to secure an agreement from the chief justice of Iraq that he would accept the class action I'd prepared on behalf of the Sunni torture victims, and that he would authorise arrests and prosecutions arising from the evidence I'd collected. This significant step forward partly made up for the fact I had to depart without seeing the people whose lives had touched mine in such a powerful way. The security situation after the Jamiat incident had made it impossible for me to leave the base, so I hadn't said any goodbyes or made last connections with those people.

But I felt no joy when I left. I flew out of Basra almost a stranger to myself. My spirit was just about broken. In the time since the incident at al-Jamiat, all the confidence and resilience I'd felt in myself then seemed to have left me. I was a different person. I didn't feel like a whole person any more.

Because I hadn't 'officially' even been at al-Jamiat, I hadn't had access to anything that might have helped me deal with it: no debrief, no counselling. There had certainly been no access to counselling or treatment in Basra; I had not been offered a debrief or even a chance to tell someone about the information I had committed to memory, which meant there was no affirmation that I had useful information to offer or that I had played an important role that day.

Even a layperson could have predicted that I was a candidate for post-traumatic stress disorder. To my mind, though, it wasn't what happened at al-Jamiat that triggered it. The fact that I'd almost died, that I'd been deprived of my liberty, that I'd been subjected to humiliation didn't do it. It was the sense of betrayal I felt from those around me afterwards that did it. I could recite everything that had happened inside and outside the police station with absolutely no problems at all, but when I began talking about the aftermath – about feeling written out of the story – I became emotional.

Even before leaving Iraq I'd started having very mixed emotions about the military I'd been serving. Part of me wanted to stay and continue the work, which I really believed in and was very important to me. But another part of me had had enough. Moreover, I was apprehensive about how life would seem back in the UK – especially since I was returning to a new husband I hadn't seen properly for seven months.

I'd had a very quick trip home in August for just eight or nine days, timed for my friends Arnie and Laura's wedding, but I didn't know how I was going to adjust to home life again – although naturally I was also very relieved to be coming back alive. By this stage the repatriation ceremonies for soldiers and officers who'd been killed in Iraq were almost biweekly, we'd lost so many lives. So I was grateful for my life and acutely aware of its preciousness. But still … I was suffering and often I couldn't even articulate why.

My feelings were intense – and they were complicated, made more so because in the weeks leading up to my departure I'd found out that my next posting was to a brand new employment law branch of the army that had been set up to promote equality and diversity in the armed forces. It seemed to me a strange place to put me after I'd gained so much operational experience. Despite the tension after the Jamiat incident, I'd really thought the army would post me somewhere in the UK or Europe in a role with an operations focus, as they had done with all my male predecessors. And apart from that, I had absolutely no experience as an employment lawyer and I would be away from the rest of the army at ALS Headquarters, in a very sleepy, isolated part of south-west England.

The usual routine upon returning home from a tour of duty is to be sent somewhere else for a few days to relax, albeit in a very controlled environment. During this time you're formally debriefed and you recover some sort of normality before returning home to your family. It was supposed to be the safest way of re-assimilating soldiers after they'd been to places like Iraq. I, however, along with a number of others, was granted a few weeks of post-operational leave but underwent no forced re-assimilation period. Most likely it didn't occur to the army that a lawyer might need re-assimilation, even one who'd been through what I'd just experienced.

We flew back in to the same military airfield from which we'd departed seven months before, RAF Brize Norton. Then we were taken by coach back to the brigade base in the south of England, where Anthony was waiting for me. I was excited, relieved and dying to see my husband, but also apprehensive, exhausted and feeling very emotional.

I was so delighted to see him, so glad to be back with the husband I loved so deeply. But I was also mentally, physically and emotionally exhausted, and at times in the days that followed I had the surreal sense of watching myself from above. Anthony was dying to talk to me and hear about everything that had happened, but now I suddenly found it impossible to speak about the Jamiat affair. I remember saying to him on a number of occasions, 'I promise I'll tell you, but you need to give me time. I want to talk about anything else but Iraq.' All I wanted to do for a while was block everything out and not talk about it or think about it – which was bizarre given it was all I could think about.

Anthony had taken some leave and we went to Egypt on holiday. It was fantastic, but it reminded me of my time in Iraq because of the desert setting and because I kept getting the same questions about my background the moment anyone heard my name. I was also still in the same state of hyper-alertness that had been the norm in Basra, and this continued for a long time after we returned to Britain. If I heard a loud noise, I'd jump. I was super-alert to movement and also very suspicious. I didn't want to see people, to the point where if someone came to the door or phoned me I couldn't bear to answer.

One day, after a few weeks of this, Anthony sat me down. 'Look,' he said, 'I need to tell you that you're not yourself. I knew you wouldn't be. I knew it would take time for you to adapt, but I'm worried about you.'

At this point I finally opened up and told him everything that had happened in Basra. He knew I'd been in al-Jamiat but he didn't know all the details, and he didn't know what had happened afterwards. He was appalled and also amazed at how much I'd had to cope with on my own, but mostly he was very upset for me and very angry.

My husband's reaction almost brought me to tears. It confirmed to me that the way I'd been treated was unacceptable – but it also triggered more emotion. I'd been trying so hard to cope with everything, but I'd been so alone in Iraq in the end except for Padre Maynard and Alex Taylor. Now, in the company of my greatest ally, something in me let go.

I didn't have much time to let go, though, as Anthony and I were due to take up new postings at the other end of England. Before that I went in for foot surgery I'd already delayed. The surgery went well, but I then became ill with bronchitis – probably because I was so run down – and this slowed the recovery process. I was also particularly concerned about a possible recurrence of lupus. Even if the lupus wasn't back in full force, it had compromised my immune system, so perhaps it played a role in my slow recovery.

Finally, in March, Anthony and I set off to take up our new posts: me at ALS Headquarters in Wiltshire, and Anthony as second in command of the air traffic control tower at RAF Brize Norton, the military base I'd flown out of and returned to after leaving Basra.

My new posting was curious as I had no experience as an employment or industrial lawyer. A newly formed branch – the first of its kind in the military – it was made up of two officers, a lieutenant colonel and a major, and we were responsible for advising on anti-discrimination, equality and diversity policies, legislation, and conducting equality training throughout the army.

Around this time I was asked by the ALS to be one of the faces for the new recruitment campaign, aimed at showing the many faces and plugging diverse recruiting in the corps.

My new posting often required me to work closely with senior Ministry of Defence personnel, drafting new legislation and policy, and to advise the Army Board on employment law matters and litigation brought by soldiers and officers against the army.

Apart from this, I started training officers and soldiers on equality and diversity (even Prince William came through as one of my 'pupils'). While the work didn't offer me the same challenges and potential achievements as human rights law, I did find it interesting.

Not long after I'd started, I discovered that James Woodham had been awarded the Military Cross. James' Military Cross citation read as follows:

In an exceptionally dangerous and unstable situation, with himself and his team held at gunpoint and threatened, Woodham provided a cool head and calm leadership, despite the imminent danger to life; one mistake could have triggered a bloodbath, but this was prevented by his courageous leadership and exceptional presence of mind in the face of extreme danger.

At the same time I found out that I'd been awarded the Queen's Commendation for Valuable Service (QCVS), which is on the same level as a Mention in Despatches, many levels below a Military Cross. Initially I assumed I'd been awarded it because of my role in the Jamiat affair. I was happy to receive an award – it was, after all, an acknowledgement that I'd been at al-Jamiat – and I appreciated the honour. But at the same time it did seem to me that James had been made the hero of the Jamiat incident.

A few months later I discovered that my citation for the QCVS was for the human rights work I'd done in Basra – well before the Jamiat incident – and that Chris Hughes had recommended me. At that point my anger began to grow at having become a ghost in the Jamiat affair.

At this stage, I was spending almost every day at work teaching soldiers how to stamp out discrimination in the armed forces. And here I was, a living example of it. What sort of hypocrite would I have been had I not fought for myself? I've always loathed injustice, but at those times when I myself have suffered it, I've never been motivated by a sense of personal indignation. My motivation has always been my complete inability to bear anything other than the truth. I've also always been acutely aware of truth of the phrase 'the personal is political' – we each need to take responsibility for what happens to us, and we each need to fight to put things right if they're not. If we don't take up this responsibility – if we don't *make* the personal political – we're letting down those who can't fight for themselves, who are unable to take responsibility because the circumstances of their lives don't enable it. I'd seen people like that – people in Iraq who had no voice and no one to fight for their rights. If I let this injustice in my own life go, I'd be betraying my own principles and all those powerless people.

In April I discovered I was three months pregnant, but it wasn't good news – a pelvic scan revealed it was an inoperable ectopic pregnancy. This meant that I had to remain pregnant for the next six months to allow my body time to reject the dangerously positioned foetus naturally. Coming on top of everything else, this heartbreaking period – when the only thing Anthony and I could think of was how our pregnancy would end – took a further toll both physically and emotionally.

It didn't change my resolve to take on the army, though. By about August, my mind was made up: I would not be a ghost any more.

CHAPTER SIXTEEN

AFTER IRAQ

Discovering that James Woodham had been recommended for the Military Cross while my own involvement in the Jamiat incident remained unrecognised galvanised me into working out the first steps towards trying to receive official recognition for the role I'd played in helping save the lives of our two SAS soldiers.

I must point out that my aim was never to seek glory. I wanted neither a Military Cross nor a public statement. All I wanted was to ensure that my role in the Jamiat incident had been included in my operational report, a type of military performance appraisal that counts towards future postings and promotion prospects. I wanted the whole truth to be told.

The obvious thing to do, in the circumstances, was seek the assistance of my colleagues in the ALS, so I went to see my commanding officer, Lieutenant Colonel Emma Peters, who like everyone else in the corps knew of my involvement in the Jamiat incident. I told her I had lots of questions for the army and that I really wanted answers. Initially she was very supportive, asking me what I wanted to get out of pursuing this matter.

'First,' I replied, 'I want to know whether any record was made of my involvement and participation in the Jamiat incident. I'd like to see a copy of my operational report to check that it was included – and, ideally, I'd also like to know why I wasn't debriefed after I got back to base. I want to know why I was treated differently from James, and why he was recommended for the Military Cross but I wasn't recognised and acknowledged.'

At this point Lieutenant Colonel Peters cautioned me. She said, very wisely, that the area of honours and awards was political, secretive and emotionally charged, and she advised me to tread carefully. People who started claiming they should have received this award or that award went out of favour very quickly, she warned. 'But let's see if we can get some answers to some other questions,' she added.

I agreed to her suggestion. For me, the award in and of itself wasn't important – but if the incident at al-Jamiat was considered important enough for James to have been awarded the Military Cross, then it really ought to be included on my operational report.

Next, I went to see the director of the ALS, Major General David Howell, and repeated what I'd already said to Lieutenant Colonel Peters. General Howell didn't see a problem with my request and replied that he was happy to write to Brigadier Lorimer on my behalf, pointing out that this matter had been troubling me – and that it was also troubling him as my general – and that we'd like clarification. We were more likely to get answers if he wrote the letter instead of me, he added. Delighted, I agreed.

General Howell duly wrote to Brigadier Lorimer, asking for a copy of my operational report. If my role hadn't been acknowledged in the report, he asked that the brigadier include it retrospectively, so the part I'd played would be formally recognised and I could keep a copy in my own files.

It took a while for the brigadier to respond. When he did, his message was as blunt as I'd learnt to expect from him. Basically, he said we couldn't have a copy of my operational report. My role in the Jamiat incident hadn't been included and he was unwilling to add it now.

Major General Howell, who must have seen how stunned I was, asked me what I wanted to do.

'It's not good enough,' I replied. 'What are my options? Can I appeal against it? Can I ask him strongly to reconsider? What can I do?'

He then told me he'd speak to Brigadier Lorimer himself and ask him to reconsider. If the brigadier agreed to include my role at the Jamiat in the report, he asked, would this be enough to satisfy me?

'If he'll acknowledge the full extent of my participation and the role I played and put that on the record in my report, and if I can then put the report in my own file, then yes,' I replied. 'It won't be on the public record, but it will be a resolution for me.'

But the brigadier still refused to grant my requests.

I had another conversation with Lieutenant Colonel Peters. She said that if I intended to keep pursuing the case, my only option was to submit a formal grievance complaint to the Army Board. She also said that if I did this – and she added that she knew she wasn't supposed to say what she was about to, particularly in our line of work – she felt compelled to warn me as my boss and as a friend that it would have an impact on my career.

'Do you really think that if I do what I believe is right, and bring to the board's attention what I believe to be discrimination that it will affect my career? Wouldn't that be discrimination in itself? Would they do that if I were a man? It really does make me wonder why we're going to so much trouble to draft anti-discrimination training packages and policies for the armed forces.' I went on, 'Doesn't it seem a bit silly to you that we're going around the country training soldiers and junior officers on equality and diversity but then we have to be quiet when discrimination happens to us? I'm afraid I can't do it. I need a resolution for my own peace of mind and I can't be a hypocrite. It's just not me.'

Lieutenant Colonel Peters repeated her warning that it would affect my career to continue down this path.

'Are you saying my career is over?' I asked.

She told me not to put words in her mouth and said she was just trying to caution me. I recognised that it was kind of her to warn me when she really didn't have to, so I backed off.

I could now see that I was in for a big fight with the army. I'd already gone to see the general's chief of staff of the ALS, Lieutenant Colonel David Wakefield, who'd been offended and affronted by my questions. He'd said in no uncertain terms that he couldn't understand what I was making a big deal about. I was a soldier and I should just let the whole thing drop. This was the culture we were fighting against in my current posting and the culture the military had to move away from if it was truly to mature and progress.

Lieutenant Colonel Wakefield was also the first person to say he thought I was medal-hunting – although he didn't say that directly to my face. He made the comment to his friend Lieutenant Colonel Peters, who told me.

I went back to see Major General Howell. 'Given the fact that Brigadier Lorimer won't amend my operational report, which is something the public will never see and will stay within the confines of my file and never be made public, and the fact that I'd be happy with that, it's not right. He's not acknowledging that I did anything and that's not acceptable to me. I can't live with it,' I said.

Major General Howell told me to be very careful. He intimated that my career would be over if I went any further with my complaint and added that he couldn't support me any longer.

And there, again, was that now-familiar twisting in my belly. 'Have you been warned, General?' I asked. 'Is there something bigger at play here?'

General Howell was silent.

Days after this last conversation with the general, I received an email advising me that, at the conclusion of my posting to the Employment Law Branch, I was to be posted back to the APA, where I'd started my ALS career and proven myself in spades. I felt like this would be taking me back to square one, sidelining me and slowing down my promotion prospects. It seemed to imply that the work I'd done in the interim meant nothing and that I was going to have to prove myself all over again.

For the first time since I'd returned from Iraq, I broke down and sobbed without stopping. I felt like I was disappearing inside this system – inside this army. I'd been excised from the Jamiat story and now it was as if my whole army career had slipped through a crack in time. If I hadn't been able to pinch my own skin and feel it hurt, I'd have wondered if I was really there at all. I'd always tried to take control of my own life, but now I felt as if I was at the mercy of forces so much bigger and more determined than me – and that they were not on my side.

One of our staff officers who worked in human resources and had signed off on my new posting arrived in my office shortly afterwards. She tried to calm me down and work out what I wanted, but I found it very difficult to express my feelings. I barely understood them myself. All I could think was that I couldn't stay a minute longer in the office. I emailed Lieutenant Colonel Peters to explain that I was in a bad way and needed to go home. I said I'd have to leave early and would let her know how I was.

It must have been about three o'clock in the afternoon. I remember driving aimlessly through the countryside for about half an hour before I parked the car in the middle of nowhere and rang Anthony.

Greatly concerned by how I sounded, he told me I definitely couldn't go back to work. 'You're going to have a mental breakdown,' he said. 'You're having an emotional breakdown now, my darling.'

I knew he was right, even though I was too distraught to really know what I was doing. But I knew I needed help. So I drove home, picked up the phone straight away, made some calls and managed to get an appointment with the local military psychiatrist the same week. This was the first time I had sought out help because it was only at this point that I realised I needed help, and realised that I couldn't tackle this problem on my own.

The psychiatrist turned out to be a charismatic, gregarious, eccentric man with absolutely no bullshit about him. When I told him my story he said he'd do everything he could to help me. It was quite strange to see how offended and infuriated he looked when I told him how I'd been treated. It was almost overwhelming to be acknowledged by someone who was hearing my story for the first time. Part of me felt that what was happening to me now was just the latest example of the army dismissing my experiences and my responses to them. It was almost as if I was being tested, to see how much I could believe in myself when almost everyone else seemed to be telling me I shouldn't. My psychiatrist's acknowledgement of my experiences was a relief. I felt like I could stop and breathe for a moment. I wasn't crazy. Something was being done to me. And it could be stopped. And should be, even if that meant my military career would be over.

I was in his office for just over an hour for that first meeting, and at the end of the appointment he took my hand

and said, 'My dear, there's nothing wrong with you. You're doing the right thing, but this thing is bigger than you or me.'

He said he was glad I knew my limits, because I was going to need help with the huge task I was about to get involved in.

It was such a big decision for me to take on this fight but by this point I was coming to the conclusion that I couldn't stay in an institution that had treated me (and others) this way and where discrimination was considered justifiable and sometimes condoned.

The psychiatrist then went on to say, and I'm paraphrasing, 'My preliminary diagnosis is that you're suffering from a form of post-traumatic stress disorder, but I don't see this as a result of the Jamiat incident and what you went through in the police station. It seems to me you've processed that very well. It's the discrimination and the injustice you experienced afterwards and are still experiencing that are causing your issues, and I think we need to get you out of harm's way and get you whatever assistance we can to help you work through that.' Then he remarked that whatever I eventually decided to do, once I'd gone through some therapy with a professional, he'd be behind me 100 per cent.

He referred me to a psychologist for some cognitive therapy. She was also fantastic and after only a couple of months I'd made such good progress that our sessions came to an end. She helped me process what had happened, then digest it and come up with a plan. And that plan was not to take the army's treatment lying down.

Throughout all our sessions, she remained completely objective. She never actively suggested one course of action or another, but she got me to the point of clarity where I was clear about my options and could make my own assessments and evaluations of which options were best for me. It's testament to her skill as a psychologist that she was able to do this even though Anthony and I were trying to deal with more terrible news.

Not long after I'd recovered from my ectopic pregnancy, Anthony was diagnosed with cancer. It was something we just weren't prepared for, having only just come to grips with a pregnancy we knew wouldn't bring us our much-longed-for baby. Anthony went on to have significant surgery, which pretty much left him immobile and without the full use of his left leg for some time. So only a short while after returning to work, I spent a number of weeks racing home at lunchtimes to help my poor husband bathe and dress himself while he convalesced.

Then came a very tense period during which we waited to see if he'd need chemotherapy. I think we both felt as if we were standing on a cliff edge. When doctors start talking to you about mortality, everything becomes slightly unreal: hearing that word while we were still a newly married couple, full of hopes and dreams, was incredibly hard.

For a while life went on hold as Anthony worked to restore his health and I supported him. At the same time, however, I began the process of submitting a formal grievance to the Army Board as well as a complaint to the Employment Tribunal of England, which was the required procedure in such cases. Strictly speaking this was an issue to do with my employment, which just happened to be in the army. I knew the risks but I wasn't afraid.

I'm not sure how, but I was able to switch emotionally from my case against the army to something far more important: Anthony's survival. The crisis in our private life only made the bond between Anthony and me stronger. We cared for each other so very much. We talked about everything. We saw each other through it all. And Anthony was extraordinary. Despite his own suffering and fears for his health, he never stopped being my greatest support.

Not long after his cancer diagnosis, we'd gone together to see my solicitor, Joanna Wade, an extremely well known employment lawyer in London. At that stage I was still agonising about mounting a legal challenge against the army and decided I wanted some advice before I made my final decision. I knew that if I elected to go down this path there was no turning back. I wasn't in conflict about this: it was more a matter of getting my head around what I knew would be the probable consequences when I did so, which took me a long time. In the end I knew I couldn't live with myself if I didn't question and challenge the way I was being treated. Anthony reminded me that if one does something for the right reasons, a good outcome will follow. I was also in a position to ensure that this didn't happen to anyone else and I felt that it was my duty and responsibility to obtain justice for myself and other silent victims in the forces.

I'd gone back to work well before the visit to Joanna and seemed to be getting the cold shoulder a little at headquarters. Some of my colleagues advised me against going down the route I was considering, no doubt realising it would end my career.

I suspect that if you asked Joanna now what she thought when she first heard my story, she'd probably admit she thought I'd embellished the tale and she couldn't believe what I was saying. So at first she seemed a little dismayed. And, honestly, if the story had been told to me I'd probably have had the same reaction. It really did seem extraordinary that I could be punished for protesting against being made to disappear from an official account.

When she realised that I wasn't embellishing the story, and that there was no other avenue available other than to lodge a formal grievance to the Army Board and a complaint to the Employment Tribunal, she agreed to represent me. She also suggested we brief a barrister to help with the litigation side of my case, since the Ministry of Defence would definitely fight it. That people from outside the army – legally qualified experts in this field, no less – were clear I really did have a strong case gave me the confidence I needed to carry on.

But before anything could go ahead, Anthony and I needed to know about his own immediate future. When the good news came through that he didn't need further treatment, I formally submitted my complaint. This was early 2007.

The army rather quickly sent me on 'gardening leave'. The walls went up and all communication stopped. There was no more contact with General Howell, Lieutenant Colonel Peters or Brigadier Lorimer, or with my friends in the ALS. I wasn't surprised. I knew by now how the army did things.

CHAPTER SEVENTEEN

DAVID AND GOLIATH

At the end of 2007 Anthony's doctors advised him that he needed no further treatment. He was told he'd need six-monthly checks for a few years, but the fact that the cancer was gone was a good enough reason for us to celebrate with a romantic holiday in Italy.

It was hard to resume the fight with the army when we returned only a week later, because we had totally switched off while in Italy. Part of me felt like packing up and going away somewhere with my husband for a very long time, so we could both catch our breath properly and rejoice in our new lease of life. But I wouldn't contemplate bowing out or backing away now.

After sending my formal grievance to the Army Board and the Employment Tribunal – before we went to Italy – I waited ... and waited ... and waited. By now Anthony and I had moved out of our married military quarters in Wiltshire.

We'd sold our house in Shropshire when we were both posted to the south of England and had eventually bought a barn and converted it into a home, in a little village called Porton, just outside the cathedral city of Salisbury.

Rather than actually gardening, I spent most of my time on military gardening leave waiting for the Ministry of Defence to respond to my grievance – and preparing for what I knew would be a fight. I had a lot to read up on, including the policies in place on promotion, postings and mental health support, as well as the policies on post-operational treatment of army personnel – and the very policies I'd been drafting on equality and diversity. I was able to put together a clear case showing that the army was breaching even its own policies.

When the army finally did respond, more than six months later, they asked for more time to get the documents they needed to fight the case. Then they started asking for extension after extension, using every excuse imaginable as to why they couldn't produce the documents to disprove my claim. Delaying tactics are common in legal matters, but when you're the one at the end of them you realise their intended effect: to put you off, to wrong-foot you, to wear you down until you either give in to what they want or give up on the whole case.

When the army eventually got back to me, they claimed I was out of time – because my complaint had to be submitted within twelve months of the final act of discrimination, which they interpreted as the Jamiat incident. This was almost amusing – there'd been acts of intimidation at Jamiat, but hardly acts of discrimination. Joanna and I prepared a counterclaim, showing that my claim had been submitted on time and that the final act of discrimination had been the Brigadier's refusal to amend my operational tour report whilst I was working in the Employment Law Branch of the ALS. Once the army accepted that my claim had in fact been in time, they continued to use delaying tactics merely to respond to our counterclaim. More months passed.

It became incredibly frustrating, because here I was sticking to time lines set by the Employment Tribunal and the Army Board to file the documents they needed from me, while there was the army seemingly able to ignore the same demands. Obviously they were dragging things out for as long as they could, no doubt hoping it would all go away. Or that I would. When they finally realised they would have to take my grievance seriously, they immediately said they would oppose it. Joanna and I had been expecting this, but I'm not sure we were expecting the army and the Ministry of Defence to start a dirty campaign to try to discredit me.

Out of the blue, a letter from the Army Medical Board arrived, asking me to produce medical reports showing I didn't have an ongoing or debilitating mental health condition. This was a tactic to have me declared medically unfit; if I was, they could say my claim should be dismissed. I'd long since stopped therapy with my psychiatrist and psychologist, but I immediately rang them and told them what had happened. Neither had been contacted by the Army Medical Board for their opinion, but both helped me greatly in proving I was far from medically unfit. Although I thought it was all outrageous, I knew it was unlikely to be the last thing the army would try in order to have the complaint dismissed or even dropped before it could start.

After they failed to have me declared medically unfit, it took months to get a date for the tribunal hearing, because the army kept delaying that, too. In the end we had to get the Employment Tribunal – which was fairly toothless – to take the Ministry of Defence to task and tell them they couldn't just keep ignoring the matter.

The day arrived when Joanna rang me and said simply, 'Well, it's finally come.' More than a year after I'd lodged my complaint, we finally had a date for the hearing, in June 2008. Then the army tried to have the date put back – which meant we had to fight their application to delay. They still didn't give up. Their next tactic was to try to have the matter heard in a closed court so the whole thing could be kept under wraps; they gave 'national security' as the reason. National security issues or not, it was obvious they wanted to keep it away from the gaze of the media and the public.

The Employment Tribunal hadn't dealt with such a political hot potato before, and of course whenever issues of national security are raised everyone gets very jittery. The Ministry of Defence was obviously hoping it could strong-arm the tribunal into having a closed court. And they would have won, too, were it not for the excellent and robust fight my barrister and solicitor put forward. Even though Karon Monahan (my barrister and a fantastic Queen's Counsel) and Joanna proved such a formidable pair, it was still a hell of a long fight against the army and the Ministry of

Defence before we won the battle to have my case heard in open court.

In the meantime, real life was turning into one of those situations where fact is stranger than fiction. Karon worked in the same legal chambers as a barrister called Cherie Booth – otherwise known as the wife of the British prime minister, Tony Blair. It was Tony Blair who'd made the decision to send British troops into Iraq; it was Tony Blair's Ministry of Defence that was fighting my claim.

In the middle of all this, Anthony and I had started IVF treatment. As anyone who has been through it knows, it's physically demanding – with rounds of appointments, daily injections, frequent blood tests and regular procedures – and gruelling, too, as it goes on for quite a while.

In April 2008 we were able to escape from the stress of it all by making a brief trip back to Perth. Debbie, one of my closest friends from law school days, was getting married and I was to be her bridesmaid. It was a godsend just to be able to switch off, even for only a fortnight, before returning to London and winding back up to prepare for my case. It was a momentous trip, because it was in Perth that we found out we were pregnant – with triplets! I let my parents know as soon as we heard the news.

I'd achieved peace of a sort with my parents two years earlier, when Anthony and I had gone back to Perth, again briefly. It was the first time we'd seen my parents since the appalling Christmas of 2003. We met them for lunch in a restaurant; they brought flowers for me, and both Mum and Dad embraced me. While there were lots of hugs and crying at lunch, it frustrated me that they could still make me feel guilty and upset – and that I, as ever, felt I could change them. I was still hoping we could be the family we were when I was younger.

So when we made the trip back in 2008, we were able to announce to Mum and Dad that they were going to be grandparents three times over. They were delighted, shocked and excited all at once. They were also nice to Anthony, who'd proved himself by now as very much on my side.

We talked little about the case I was bringing against the army. I think my parents felt unqualified – for the first time – to comment about it. They also resisted reminding me they hadn't been keen on me joining the army in the first place. Anthony and I left Perth feeling we'd put the relationship with my parents on a firmer footing, and we were excited about being able to make them grandparents.

*

Back in the UK, there was no forgetting the battle that loomed ahead. I found myself wondering more than ever why the army remained so determined, three years later, to leave me out of the Jamiat affair. Why the desperation to pretend I had never been involved or had played an inconsequential role? I'd followed an order to go to the Jamiat, where I'd risked my own life to rescue Ed and Di – just like James Woodham and the SAS team who'd tried to sneak into the police compound. And my life had indeed been in the balance, just as theirs had been.

In this day and age, was this all really a case of ridiculous, old-fashioned sexism tied to pride and tradition? Was there something about army culture I didn't understand? In the eyes of the army, could only a soldier – never a military lawyer – be recognised for valour in the field? After almost three years, surely it wouldn't create too much of a stir if the public learnt the truth? And was it the case that the army was still so traumatised by its failure in Basra that it didn't want to remind the public – and the media – what had happened that day at the Jamiat? If so, why didn't it simply agree to my first, very simple request: to amend my operational report and include the part I'd played in the events that day? If they'd done that, I wouldn't be taking them to court now.

There was one last attempt to frighten me off, and I suppose I should have seen it coming. The weekend before my hearing, an article was published in the English newspaper *The Telegraph* publicising my case and sarcastically using the term 'hero' in the headline. The crux of the piece was insulting and totally untrue – it was written very much along the lines of 'female lawyer seeks ridiculous amount of money'. I think it even stated some ludicrous sum I was meant to be demanding. It was nasty, and it hurt, because obviously the intention was to portray me as acting purely for my own glory and monetary gain. I could only guess at who was behind it, but not many people knew the details of my case. I certainly hadn't spoken to any journalists and nor would I have, especially since I was still a serving officer in the armed forces.

Inevitably, the article partially succeeded in turning forces personnel and some members of the public against me.

The internet comments made for very unpleasant reading, their gist being 'How dare this woman ask for so much money when we've got soldiers coming back with no arms and legs who are having to fight for compensation?'

The compensation claim I was making as part of my formal grievance was based on constructive dismissal, as it had been made clear I'd have no future in the army after the case. It was based on my loss of future earnings, since I had a guaranteed commission for at least another ten or twelve years. In fact, my claim was very conservative because I'd based it on being promoted only one further rank – whereas, realistically, I'd probably have been promoted two more ranks if I'd remained in the army as a military lawyer and been treated fairly. I wasn't trying to bleed the army, and I wanted people to understand that the case I was fighting wasn't about the money. If I'd been in it for the money, I would have let the army medically retire me and taken a pension for life. That would have been the easier option.

Nor was I doing this to make a point. Justice was on the line. *The truth* was on the line. That was what I wanted, more than anything. When I'd taken a commission in the army I'd committed myself to serve the British people. I'd done that to the best of my ability and taken great risks to do so. The other men and women who were with me in Basra had done the same at various times. If all we were doing was serving in an army that disregarded the truth then I wasn't sure what any of us were doing in it.

The day after the article came out, Anthony and I discovered that a journalist had visited a couple of our neighbours asking questions about me. We then went around our little cul-de-sac and knocked on everyone's front door to ask them to let us know if they were approached by the media.

At one stage when we went out to the shops we were followed by a car with photographers inside. They'd been parked at the end of our street. At home, the phone rang continuously, and we were bombarded by emails from more journalists. My solicitor soon let us know she was getting badgered as well. We spent the weekend saying, 'No comment.' That is, at least, when we occasionally answered the phone.

Anthony was becoming very concerned, and even more protective of me because of my pregnancy, which at this stage was still a secret. We hadn't even told my solicitor and barrister the news. The last thing I needed was to let myself be harassed by the media. The little lives growing inside me were uppermost in our minds.

The night before my case was due to be heard, Anthony and I packed the car and started the drive up to London.

CHAPTER EIGHTEEN

D-DAY

I felt sick with nerves when I woke up the next morning in the hotel where Anthony and I were staying. It was a hot English summer's day, but I was barely aware of the idyllic weather outside. In a few hours' time my case was due to begin.

Despite my jitters, I was psyched up and more than ready to give evidence. I was also absolutely determined not to let the lawyers representing the army and the Ministry of Defence intimidate me – as I fully expected them to try. On the contrary, I intended to make very plain my memories of what went on inside the Jamiat on that day, three years earlier – which, as it turned out, had been one of Britain's most significant incidents during the occupation of Basra.

Anthony and I took a taxi to the café where we were meeting my barrister and solicitor, which was just along from the Employment Tribunal building in Holborn, London.

Karon and Joanna were already there when we arrived. The moment we walked in, I could see they had something important to tell us.

'We need to prepare you,' they said. 'There's a huge press contingent waiting for you at the court.'

I'd thought a few journalists would turn up because of *The Telegraph* article, but didn't expect that much interest. Now I had to prepare for the full glare of media attention. Having had no experience of it, I didn't really know what to expect.

When it was time to walk across to the tribunal, we were suddenly rushed by about two dozen journalists and surrounded by photographers and camera operators. Whoever had leaked the information about my case to *The Telegraph* hadn't engaged in the cleverest exercise in strategic thinking. The article had served only to bring attention to the case, and they couldn't control what happened after that.

I didn't speak to any of the journalists as they formed a pack around Anthony, Joanna, Karon and me. I just tried to keep my pace, and my gaze, steady. The journalists followed us into the building, where officials quickly took the four of us upstairs to a room made available for us to wait in until it was time for our case. The journalists and photographers camped out on the floor in the lobby. Clearly, they were staying for the duration. And my sense of incredulity was staying, too.

Now that we were sequestered away from the media, I prepared myself for the moment I'd have to stand up in court and start giving evidence. Courts are intimidating enough when you're a lawyer appearing for a client; they are even more so when you *are* the client.

As we waited, we were all startled by a sudden knock at the door and opened it to find a fairly young, nervous-looking barrister standing outside in the hall. He asked to speak to my barrister outside and in only a few minutes she returned with the message that the Ministry of Defence wanted to settle.

I really wasn't sure how to feel about this. I was still completely psyched up to fight my case – I was coiled, almost ready for battle. My barrister was also completely committed to the fight. It's true she'd prepared me for the possibility they might want to settle, but that was before all the media interest had been sparked in my case. When we heard nothing more after the story in *The Telegraph*, we assumed the Ministry of Defence had decided against trying to do any sort of deal. Now, at the eleventh hour, they'd caved in, but it brought me no joy. In fact, it made me really angry. All I could think was they could have settled months earlier; indeed, this whole issue could have been resolved so easily and quickly two years before.

'Tell them they can go to hell,' I said to Joanna. 'This isn't about the money. I want the press downstairs and the public to know my story, and to know what the army has done.'

The army had put me through hell for years now; they'd had plenty of opportunities to resolve the entire matter at a very low level, when no one would have known a thing about it. Instead, they'd tried to discredit me. They'd tried scare tactics. They'd tried to get rid of my case through thoroughly underhand means. I was not an enemy combatant. I was not even trying to bring them into disrepute. All I was trying to do was have them correct my operational record. It hadn't seemed a big request when I first made it, and it didn't seem like one now, certainly not one warranting the ordeal my husband and I had been through. What they'd done wasn't right, and I wasn't going to let them slip out of it so easily.

My barrister went back to the Ministry of Defence lawyer waiting outside in the hall and told him my response: 'No deal.'

Once the ministry's lawyer had delivered this message, however, Joanna sat me down to discuss the situation further. During our conversation, she suggested I rethink the offer to settle. 'You could get an apology out of them, and they'll certainly learn lessons from this,' she said. 'You could get some sort of settlement to help you move on.'

Joanna was an excellent solicitor. She was trying to give me very balanced advice, especially as she was aware I was already being headhunted for other jobs. This tempered her advice, as it seemed clear that while my military career was over, I would still have a future career in the law, so all was not lost. But, at the same time, I knew Karon was very much looking forward to representing me in court and cross-examining some of the army's witnesses, who'd made out in their statements that I was a disgruntled officer who'd gone off the rails a bit after the Jamiat incident. The gist of their statements was that after Jamiat I was no longer motivated or operating to the fullest of my abilities. Even if that were the case, it wouldn't have taken a psychology degree to understand that anyone who'd had an experience like Jamiat would be dealing with repercussions – their mood would be affected, for example. It wouldn't necessarily mean their job performance suffered.

Obviously I'd seen these witness statements beforehand, during the disclosure process. Of course, none of the army's witnesses denied the simple fact that I'd been at the Jamiat – they all knew I'd been there. Had they tried to deny it, they would have perjured themselves, and I knew they weren't about to do that.

I can't remember if I saw a statement from James Woodham, although I believe he'd been asked to minimise my involvement in what happened. He'd also denied standing behind me when the man with the AK47 cocked his weapon at us. The other witnesses included John Lorimer, David Howell, David Wakefield and Emma Peters, all senior army officers. Now they were all in the building, although we'd been put on different floors – and at opposite ends of those floors. At one stage I went to the toilet, where I ran into Emma Peters. She left the moment she saw me without saying a word. I also said nothing.

I had just three witnesses: the padre, and my psychiatrist and psychologist. I didn't need a whole team of people, because we felt that my telling the story about what had happened to me was powerful enough in itself. While I had to demonstrate and provide sufficient evidence of discrimination, it was up to the army and the Ministry of Defence to disprove it. The whole exercise was meant to expose the flaws in the army's version of events. We were also relying heavily on documentary evidence proving I'd been at the Jamiat – and, of course, we had the anti-discrimination policy and legislation on our side as well, given this was still an Employment Tribunal case.

So there were a lot of reasons why I wasn't prepared to settle at this stage. As a lawyer myself, I know that the role of a solicitor is to maintain a degree of independence, listening to reason and offering perspective. Both Joanna and Karon certainly did this, but it was also very clear that they absolutely believed in my case. They were passionate about it, in fact. So as far as I was concerned we were all up for a fight.

Equally, though – as became increasingly obvious – the Ministry of Defence was desperate to settle. *Really* desperate: over the course of the next four or five hours, the same junior barrister went backwards and forwards between our two floors, carrying messages between our side and his. The army kept upping the offers and adding new conditions they thought would make the deal more palatable for me. As the hours passed and these negotiations continued, I began to get exhausted – and emotional, too.

Downstairs, the press were getting itchy feet. Messages kept arriving from journalists wanting to know what was going on. Everything was obviously building to a climax and at this point Anthony told me we would have to let Joanna and Karon know I was pregnant. So I told them my news – adding that I was expecting triplets. This was a major turning point for both of them. They proceeded to have a long, intense conversation with me.

'I'd love to fight this for you. I'd love to have a go at this,' said Karon, 'but just by getting to this point, you've won. With them now trying so hard to settle, you've won. The power is still with us. Don't see this as a compromise or a loss. This is an absolute win.' She added that there were still ways and means for me to tell my story publicly and added that we could put some conditions on the terms of settlement so that lessons would be learnt in the army. 'There will be an apology and an acknowledgement of the part you played in the whole affair, and that, don't forget, is what you set out to achieve by doing all of this,' she reminded me.

Karon spoke a lot of sense and, as she was talking, something clicked. My babies had never really left my mind, but the paramount importance of looking after the precious little souls inside me hit home at this moment. I knew it was time to look at the bigger picture: the health of the children Anthony and I would soon have.

By now it was getting late in the day. It was clear that if we turned down the offer to settle, I'd probably be on the stand for the next two or three days giving evidence. Karon and Joanna were very worried about this, now that they knew about my pregnancy. Indeed, they'd suddenly become exceedingly protective. If I went to get a drink or needed to go to the toilet, they made sure someone accompanied me. There was something almost poetic about the situation, I thought. Three women – all lawyers, one pregnant – and all of us fighting one of the most powerful, and traditionally masculine, institutions in the land.

It was true, as they said, that everything I'd set out to do I could now achieve without putting our unborn babies at risk. If I didn't take this opportunity – if I continued with the case just for the opportunity to give evidence in court – I was probably being very selfish. I suspect now that I'd realised this the moment the Ministry of Defence barrister arrived at the door with the first offer to settle. It's just that it took me a while to get to the stage where I was ready to agree to negotiate.

Between us, we wrote up the conditions. I wanted an apology from the highest officer in the armed forces, the chief of the general staff, General Sir Richard Dannatt. I set out exactly what I wanted in this written apology – which was also to be a public apology. I wanted an assurance that the army was going to make systemic changes based on my case and, most importantly, an acknowledgement of the part I'd played in trying to get our two SAS men released on 19 September 2005. Part of the letter General Dannatt eventually wrote read, 'The Army will consider carefully your perception of the way that you were treated in the period that followed the Jamiat incident with a view to ensuring that appropriate lessons are learned.' There was obviously the monetary settlement as well, but more than that I wanted an assurance that the army would conduct a review into what had happened and that no other member of the armed forces would be subjected to the same treatment I'd received. I wouldn't know what the outcome of the review was, as I wasn't allowed to have access to it, but I hoped that it would address the issue of post-operational briefing and mental health procedures for all. I also hoped that it would recognise the role women were, in reality, playing in Iraq and Afghanistan. This later turned out to be the case.

Of course, I had to agree to a couple of their demands, too. I wasn't allowed to talk publicly about the monetary settlement, or about issues involving national security, neither of which I'd have done in any case. They could have tried for some gag clauses to stop me saying anything at all, but my legal team was very clever in how it framed what we would and would not accept. As Karon had already said, there were other ways my story could come out in public.

Our biggest advantage was that the army fervently wanted the whole thing to just go away, although they agreed I could read a prepared statement to the media. It had been made clear to all of us that the journalists weren't going away otherwise, so this was a practical step. There was no statement from the Ministry of Defence, which never made public statements in such cases as mine and would never admit liability – despite the fact that to all intents and purposes I had won against them.

Anthony, Joanna, Karon and I went downstairs into the foyer so I could make my statement. Journalists came from everywhere the moment we got out of the lift.

'Rabia will provide you with a statement but she won't take questions after that. Please respect her wishes,' said Joanna.

I gave my statement and of course they still asked me lots of questions, shouting over each other to be heard. 'I'm sorry,' I told them. 'I can't take any questions because I'm still a serving officer. I'm sure you'll all understand.'

And then my heart leapt, because I could hear people calling out, 'Well done, Rabia! Good for you!'

The encouraging comments kept coming as we walked through the foyer and out of the building, surrounded by journalists who continued to walk with us for several more steps. At the end of the street Anthony and I hugged Karon and Joanna goodbye before we returned to our hotel. I felt only relief. I'd thought I wanted my day in court – to have my say in front of the people who'd denied it to me in the past – but in the end that didn't matter. What I'd really wanted was for the truth to be told – I wanted to have an accurate record of my service. Now, at last, I would.

Anthony took my hand and we walked away from the media, the tribunal – and the past.

CHAPTER NINETEEN

PROSECUTING TERRORISTS

While I was still on gardening leave, in the weeks leading up to my court case, I'd received a phone call. The caller, a headhunter in London, had a fascinating job proposal: to work for the Counter Terrorism Division (CTD) of the England and Wales Crown Prosecution Service (CPS).

'Your timing couldn't be more perfect,' I'd said immediately.

Naturally, I was curious to know how he'd heard about me. His answer was simple: through people who knew of my role in Iraq and had recommended me for the position. He didn't name the person or people who'd recommended me, and to this day I still have no idea, because I worked with so many people in Iraq, both military and non-military, including those from the Red Cross and the British consul's office.

I told him I was definitely interested, and a couple of informal meetings were quickly set up, which is when I first met Sue Hemming, the amazing woman heading up the CTD.

Sue was on the panel of people who later interviewed me, and after two rounds I was offered the job as crown advocate with the division. Obviously, though, I couldn't take up this position until I'd resigned my commission in the army.

I was very honest from the start about everything that was happening. Sue Hemming told me she'd already heard about my battle with the army, before adding that as far as she could tell, I had a strong case. She also said that she admired and respected me for what I was doing but it had absolutely no bearing on the fact they wanted me for the job. It was such a relief to hear this, and to feel I was among professionals and grown-ups again.

After that it was merely a matter of waiting for the resignation paperwork to go through before I started work at the CTD in London. When the army decided to settle, it meant that I became a free agent sooner than expected. Winning this very high-profile case had attracted a lot of attention, and several good newspaper articles reported the outcome, written by journalists who'd called out their congratulations to me on the day. June hadn't yet ended when I started work at the CPS.

By then I'd also received a letter from David Howell, the director general of the ALS, providing me with a very positive testimonial; this had been another condition of settlement. On my part, I agreed to retire from the army voluntarily and honourably. None of the people in the army who'd distanced themselves from my case ever contacted me again. My former boss, Lieutenant Colonel Dick Pierce, now retired, was an exception. He was always very supportive and has kept in touch. I also received an email from James Woodham – a long time after I'd written to him in 2006 to congratulate him on his Military Cross.

James contacted me because he'd been approached by the author of a book supported by the Ministry of Defence. It was to be a collection of interviews with some of the heroes of the Iraq and Afghanistan campaigns. James wanted my permission to include some details of what I'd done on the day of the Jamiat incident in the chapter dedicated to him. He told me he'd felt embarrassed about being singled out and awarded the Military Cross, and that he wanted to make it clear in the book that it was the efforts of others, not just his, that saved lives on that fateful day in Basra. This was gratifying.

I loved my new job at the CTD, but Anthony was now being given the cold shoulder at work. It was made clear to him by his new RAF commanding officer that he wasn't going anywhere in his career and that by publicly supporting me he'd made life difficult for himself. My husband was posted two and a half hours away from where we were living and was refused a posting closer to home, despite the fact we were going to have triplets. It started to feel a bit like we'd won the battle but lost the war.

For me, however, there was a seamless transition to my new job. I moved from interesting, challenging work to a job that made me feel I was playing an even more important part in the fight against the extremism, terrorism and violence now taking place on a large scale. Having faced the heartbreak of being forced to leave a career in the military

I thought I'd be continuing for some time, I could never have guessed that my departure would open doors to something even more meaningful, challenging and fulfilling. The military had always been a means to an end – now I was doing exactly what I'd dreamt of all those years ago when I left Australia for the UK.

My work at the CTD essentially involved advising on and preparing prosecutions for terrorism offences, as well as offences against the Official Secrets Act (read: rogue spies). Hijacking and piracy offences also came into my sphere, as well as violent extremism – or race hate crimes, as they're more widely known – plus war crimes, and crimes against humanity. I appeared in various courts including the Old Bailey for extradition matters and sentencing hearings. We had the world's best barristers at hand for the high-profile terrorism trials, in which I played the role of instructing solicitor.

For obvious reasons I can't talk in detail about a lot of my work, especially those cases and investigations that are still ongoing. But as an example, one case involved potential Official Secrets Act offences by someone who'd served with the Special Forces. It was wonderful to be doing this work and fulfilling my lifelong dream of fighting intolerance and bigotry, standing up for the ordinary people who so often had no voice and protecting my fellow citizens from terrorism.

Because of my time in Iraq and in the military, I quickly became a specialist in these areas and ended up being referred a lot of Ministry of Defence cases involving potential war crimes prosecutions – as well as cases involving military personnel who'd allegedly committed offences of the nature we were dealing with at the CTD. At one point I advised on potential war crimes offences against some military personnel who'd served in Afghanistan and Iraq – an irony if there ever was one!

I was also responsible for advising on some cases involving former Northern Ireland terrorists who'd been released years earlier as part of the Good Friday Agreement, after we'd received intelligence they were becoming active again. So I'd come almost full circle after my first tour of duty there years earlier with the army.

For me, though, the most memorable part of my time at the CTD was when I became the prosecuting officer in a big terrorism case we referred to as the 'Bookshop Case', involving a man we called 'the al-Qaeda Librarian'. This man was responsible for distributing and selling the largest amount of al-Qaeda- and terrorism-related material on the internet, and in print, that the world had ever seen.

I'd quickly discovered as a result of my job that people like the Librarian, who were influential in recruiting, brainwashing and radicalising young people, had great charisma, intelligence and presence. It was no accident that they were able to recruit young people, mostly men, to their cause. In the main they were also well educated, and many were very technologically or computer savvy. Very often, they were IT experts. They'd all gone through a period of isolation or alienation in their lives, and it was usually during that period that they'd either been recruited or turned themselves to radicalism. The British Muslim youth provided a breeding ground for terrorist organisations. You only had to go to places in Bradford or the West Midlands or South London to see it.

When it came to the al-Qaeda Librarian, I was particularly struck by his presence. He was extremely tall, with long hair and a very long beard – and he was absolutely steely. The only time I saw him was in a courtroom setting, although it wasn't my job to question him. My role was to work closely with the Counter Terrorism Command police, or SO15, in preparing the case for trial, to advise them about the charges they could lay, and then to instruct our QC and junior counsel.

This meant spending days reviewing the evidence, which included watching video recordings of interviews the police had conducted with this man. I also had to be familiar with all the evidence and with the material he'd allegedly posted on the internet and sold and distributed around the globe. Inevitably, it meant I had to watch the most atrocious material of all: video clip after video clip of beheadings and brutal murders, all posted with the intent of exciting and tantalising dangerous radicals.

This part of the job was horrific, although it came later, after I'd given birth to our triplets. I was protected from the worst of the material while I was still pregnant. There was an excellent support network at the CTD, in which I'd include many of the police officers with whom I became good buddies. We all turned to each other on a regular basis to download, although the police, in particular, were extremely alert to the pressures and traumas of our work. I guess they were so much more switched on to it because of all the dreadful events they had to deal with.

So in terms of employee health and welfare, there was nothing but wonderful treatment. And the police I worked so closely with, the majority of whom were male officers, made sure there was always someone with me whenever I was viewing this ghastly stuff. They also made sure someone would take me out of the room for a break once in a while. They brought me coffees and lunch. I was very grateful to them for the way they got me through it.

There was no way around viewing the videos, though. I knew I had to see them in order to get a sense of the true criminality of the Librarian's acts. Beheadings are barbaric. They're not swift. They're horrific and very, very difficult to watch. It's certainly nothing like in the movies, where it's one clean strike or slice through the neck. It's absolutely gruesome. Thankfully, I had a two-hour drive back home to Wiltshire every day, and on the way home I'd work on trying to forget what I'd seen.

Viewing the dreadful material being distributed on the internet was very unsettling for another reason as well. In Basra I'd wished I'd known more about Islam and Islamic culture after I met such fine examples of young Muslim people, but now, back in the UK, it was awful to see the corruption of Islam – and Muslims – and how horribly misguided, dangerous extremists had blackened the name of Islamic culture. At the same time, though, I absolutely did not relate to any of the people involved in the ugliness of 'Islamic' extremism. To me they were nothing but terrorists – criminals of the worst kind.

I didn't feel I had to educate my colleagues that the material put out by people like the Librarian wasn't the work of Islam.

This was because I was working in central, cosmopolitan London, where a number of my colleagues were themselves Muslims. I was working with a group of enlightened, highly educated people who were at the top of their game. Every day I was spending my time with a really intelligent, worldly, wise bunch of people. I'd left the male-dominated, white Anglo-Saxon environment of the army far behind.

One former senior prosecutor in the CPS had taken on the role of setting up community engagement initiatives. He approached me not long after I arrived and asked me to get involved in this program. As it happened, I'd already suggested to management that they might use my background and experience in this way, because there was a real drive within the division to educate the community. The idea was that we helped the police educate Muslim communities, in particular, about the fact that we weren't targeting Islam and Muslims but were targeting the reality that some Muslims were being recruited as well as the way they were being recruited.

But we also wanted to tell people about the work we did in the CTD, and the fact that a large amount of it involved prosecuting not Muslims but violent extremists, often from white supremacist groups. For this reason, a decision had been made by the CPS to have open and transparent reporting. I helped create the CTD website, especially the section where we published all our case results openly.

The terrorism cases that came along did take a lot of our time, but in actual fact our work dealt increasingly with violent extremism cases – the racial hatred offences. The far-right and Neo-Nazi groups were, sadly, a growth area. Many prosecutions came out of their activities. The far right and the hate offenders tended not to be particularly educated, intelligent or sophisticated, and they usually came from very troubled, violent backgrounds. A lot of them abused alcohol and drugs, too. In their own way they were just as dangerous and lethal as the Islamic radicals.

It wasn't as hard as I feared to get the message across to the Muslim communities, because I found that a lot of the imams who were normally the community's leaders were very switched-on people and extremely supportive of what we were trying to do. As ever, success in such instances is all about people skills and showing respect to the communities – although some Muslims who attended our meetings were totally unreceptive.

The vocal ones were usually the younger ones, those we could see would be the future prime targets for radical groups, if they weren't members of those groups already. They would give us a look of complete disdain and disrespect – a look they had down pat. We could tell what they were thinking just by looking at them.

It was depressing and disturbing, but it was countered by a wonderful Muslim Police Forum I attended. Excluding my time in Iraq, it was the first time I'd found myself in a professional environment with such a large group of Muslims – there were probably about 200 of us altogether – and a group with so many women. A lot of the women were wearing either hijabs or burqas and, to be honest, that challenged some of my own preconceptions, because

I remember being struck by how liberal, funny and similar to me they were. And why wouldn't they be? Just like Nour, they were modern, professional women who also happened to be Muslim.

I didn't get the chance to attend any mixed- or multi-faith community meetings as part of the community engagement initiative. The gulf that has grown between Christians and Jews on one side and Muslims on the other as a result of Islamic extremism is a crisis for us all. I felt strongly that the work we were doing was making a change within neighbourhoods where suspicion too often led to hatred and ultimately violence. It's such a simple thing to do, to sit down and talk with other people, find common ground and make them feel included, but it's also vital, because stopping extremism begins in those communities. If people feel we're shutting them out, they'll remain silent as their children walk into traps set for them by men like the al-Qaeda Librarian.

I hope with all my heart and soul that the community engagement program is continuing to make inroads in those neighbourhoods. But it was still at a fledging stage when I made another major decision and resigned from my job in March 2011.

CHAPTER TWENTY

MOTHERHOOD AND THE FUTURE

It was motherhood, not Iraqi insurgents in Basra or terror-ists in Britain, that turned me into a lioness overnight. I simply wasn't prepared for the intensity of love I felt for our boys when they finally came into the world eight weeks early, on 24 October 2008. It's a love that's almost ferocious, in the sense that I know I'd protect to the death these children who immediately became the focus of our lives.

I had a very healthy pregnancy. I worked until about twenty-eight or twenty-nine weeks, when I was almost waddling because I'd become so humungous. 'Are you crazy? Enough!' my doctor finally said, ordering me home to rest. Up to that point I'd been walking, swimming and still attending Pilates classes – all the while doing the four-hour return journey from Wiltshire to the office in London each day.

Anthony and I had absolute faith and confidence that I'd give birth to three healthy babies. We were certain that this was our destiny – and perhaps even the reward and the blessing for everything that we'd endured as a couple, and that I'd been through on my own. It's just as well that we were both so serene, because the medical specialists keeping close watch over my pregnancy regularly warned us of all the risks and dire consequences that being pregnant with triplets can involve. I listened to them, of course, but I felt so well I didn't think I needed to worry so much.

At one stage we were referred to a Harley Street specialist, probably the world expert on a potentially dangerous condition called twin-to-twin transfusion syndrome, which can develop in the early stages of pregnancy. Essentially, the blood flow can become uneven between identical twins who share a placenta, meaning one twin gets an oversupply while the other doesn't get enough. Given that we had an identical set of twins as part of the triplet 'package', and that twin-to-twin transfusion syndrome did indeed show up early on in my pregnancy, we were very fortunate to be referred to this man.

During one of our first appointments with him we learnt that the condition seemed to be getting worse. It can self-correct or it can do the opposite, and in the worst-case scenario it can lead to the death of one twin, both twins or, in the case of triplets, all three infants. It can also lead to serious problems such as developmental retardation and brain damage. The specialist wanted to do an amniocentesis to see exactly how bad things were, and also to check whether one or more of the triplets was showing signs of Down Syndrome. He also canvassed the possibility of invasive in-utero laser surgery down the track if necessary, a procedure that carried with it a risk of losing all three babies (as would leaving the condition untreated in this situation).

The focus of the medical approach was on saving the non-twin baby, Aaron. He'd been assessed as having the greatest chance of survival, so if push came to shove they would try to get at least one healthy baby out of this. Anthony and I were totally convinced, however, that all three babies would be healthy and so we didn't want to intervene until it was absolutely necessary. Luckily, the condition righted itself within a couple of months, so we were never forced to make any difficult decisions.

At thirty-two and a half weeks I went into spontaneous labour the evening before I was due for a hospital check-up. I'd physically run out of room in my womb. The magic number for me had been thirty weeks, as once my pregnancy went past that I knew I'd be allowed to have my babies in the district hospital in Wiltshire instead of having to travel up to London. I'd have loved to have got to the thirty-four weeks considered full term in the case of most triplet pregnancies, but that wasn't to be.

The baby who triggered my labour was Aaron – which made perfect sense later on, because Aaron has turned out to be the most vocal of our three boys, and the ringleader when they get up to mischief. He's also the boss when they're playing and has taken after me by being quite impatient.

It truly was a delivery theatre when the boys made their entrance, because along with their parents there was quite an audience to greet them. We had just over twenty medics present, including three obstetricians, a paediatric team for each baby and the neonatal nurses. I couldn't have a natural birth, but that didn't matter in the least. The only important thing was making sure the children had the very best chance. It was lovely how things turned out, because the consultant obstetrician on duty the day I went into labour was an Australian doctor on exchange from Sydney. It seemed perfect that an Aussie was delivering my three little Anglo-Australian babies.

The boys hadn't learnt how to keep an audience waiting in anticipation, though. When the great moment came, it was very quick. I had a spinal block, my Aussie obstetrician performed a caesarean and within five minutes, to the sounds of music we had carefully chosen, the boys were born, one minute apart. Our boys! Our children! Weighing in between three and four pounds, they were finally here and we were thrilled, relieved and so thankful.

We'd come up with a shortlist of names, but as soon as we set eyes on them we knew who they were and named them straight away: Aaron, Noah and Oscar. Within seconds, though, the boys were whisked away to the neonatal intensive care unit, because they were a little unwell and vulnerable, being so premature. It was hard not being able to hold them in my arms immediately after they were born. The first I eventually got to hold was Oscar, two days after the birth.

Anthony was an absolute star. For the first twenty-four hours after delivery, because I was still affected by anaesthetic, I wasn't allowed to move around. I was desperate for Anthony to carry me, wheel me – do anything to get me into the neonatal intensive care unit to see our children! He was literally running from one end of the hospital to the other, taking photos, getting little handprints, doing everything he could to make me feel close to them.

I was discharged after ten days, but the boys had to remain where they were, and it was five weeks before we were allowed to take them home. Two of them needed oxygen and help with their breathing, they all needed help with feeding – and they all needed to put on weight.

I understood, of course, that they had to stay in hospital for the short term, but it still felt counterintuitive to give birth and then come home from hospital without my babies. I yearned for them each time we left the hospital grounds. Anthony and I would go home late at night to do some washing and get some rest – before turning around and going straight back to hospital, where we spent all day and most of the night with our boys.

Anthony's new commanding officer gave him grief over his request for paternity leave – despite knowing our babies were in specialist care – but Anthony ultimately managed to get some paternity leave and to take some unused annual leave. I simply couldn't have managed those first few weeks on my own, and neither of us was in any emotional state to be away from the boys or each other.

Finally, to our huge joy, the great day arrived: our boys came home – and on my birthday, 25 November. After that, our lives were turned upside down, although we'd known this would be the case, especially as we had no family or close friends living nearby. Nevertheless, it was a change we accepted without question. People talk about the instant bond between parents and children, and that was certainly the case with us. We fell in love with the boys the minute we saw them, and that love intensified each day.

Family and close friends were desperate to see the boys, so the first few weeks at home were filled with visits and presents for our threesome. My parents were due to come and stay with us for the festive season. Anthony and I had great fun in the meantime, preparing for the boys' first Christmas. Three little Christmas stockings, three hand-painted Christmas tree baubles and, of course, three special Christmas outfits. The Christmas spirit truly was in abundance at our place that year!

My parents arrived on 23 December but sadly, after only two or three days, my father had to rush off to the US because his younger brother, who was holidaying there, had died. My mother stayed on with us, although she didn't change as many nappies or do as much to help as I'd expected, especially given Anthony and I were so flat out with our three tiny babies.

Unfortunately, though, Anthony's situation at work worsened during this time. Because of the difficulties he was experiencing, he became depressed and totally disillusioned with the RAF and the armed forces in general. He resigned a few weeks after the children were born. Resigning was a bigger deal for him than it had been for me, because the RAF had been his life. I'd had a great career before I joined the armed forces, whereas for a while he'd been the youngest RAF officer in the UK, after fulfilling a long-held dream and joining up straight after he'd left school.

So for him this was more than just leaving a job – it was leaving a lifestyle, a career and a dream. Watching him go through it was heartbreaking for me, because I knew that were it not for the case I'd brought against the army – and the support Anthony had given me – he'd have continued his very promising career as an officer.

Combined with the emotional exhaustion after the case was over and being new parents of triplets, Anthony's problems at work really took a lot out of us. But at the same time it made our partnership even stronger, if that's possible. We really did become an invincible couple.

Anthony triumphed in the short term, though. Not long after he left the RAF, an excellent management position came up in the operational development area of the British Airport Authority. He got the job easily. He was based at Heathrow and was responsible for all of the authority's airports, so he also got to travel a fair bit. So we went onwards and upwards, and for both of us our new jobs were so similar to our previous occupations that neither involved a difficult transition.

Something else happened that December. There wasn't enough room for all the children's clothes and toys in the house after they were born. So one cold, brisk afternoon, not long after Anthony had resigned from the RAF, we decided that this was the moment to pack our uniforms and military kit away in boxes and store them in the shed. It really felt like we were closing the door on such a huge chapter in our lives. Afterwards, still in the shed, we embraced for a long time. We both shed tears.

Then we suddenly heard one of the babies cry, and we raced back inside the house.

*

Love for the boys inevitably led to the dilemma many professional parents face. I felt guilty about going back to work, and I worked for only three days a week for the first two years when I'd have much preferred to spend all my time with our precious children. At the same time, though, I was completely committed to a job I passionately believed in. Anthony loved his new job as well. Career-wise, we were both where we wanted to be, and there was no point denying this.

The long commute to London from Wiltshire didn't make things any easier – although, thank goodness, we were able to employ a wonderful nanny to help with the boys and she remains a friend to this day. We realised how fortunate we were to be able to afford this kind of help and never took it for granted. Having triplets is certainly a handful – my husband and I often jokingly say that were it not for our military training we would never have coped anywhere near as well. It almost made sense that if anyone was going to have triplets, it would be two people who'd been in the armed forces.

Increasingly, we thought about the future and over the next two years kept wrestling with the idea of leaving the UK and moving to Australia. Despite everything that had happened in the past, I'd become homesick. More importantly, after the boys were born we'd gone through three long, harsh winters. The children often fell ill with chest infections and breathing problems, and they were in and out of hospital quite a bit. By the time they turned two, we'd reached a point where we realised that the future was about them, not us. We knew we'd been incredibly lucky to have such exciting careers and to have realised our ambitions, but we really had to put the boys first.

By this time Britain had become a gloomy place to live. The Global Financial Crisis had hit hard, people were being made redundant everywhere, businesses were going to the wall and the property market was in dire straits. We'd tried to sell our own home in Wiltshire in order to cut down on our commuting hours, but the house had been on the market for ages and we were forced to move to Surrey to be closer to work and rent out the Wiltshire barn until it eventually sold in 2011.

Undoubtedly, though, the weather was the clincher. When you've got three little boys who are getting more and more active and it's cold and wet and dark a lot of the time, that's challenging! Ultimately, we decided to make a move sooner rather than later, while they were still at an age at which they could adjust to the life and lifestyle we wanted them to have, and wouldn't be leaving friends behind. Nor would their education be affected.

For me, something else was driving the decision to leave Britain. At work I faced a daily diet of horror of a kind that can make you look at life – and the world – very differently. I was always hyper-alert, waiting for the next act of terrorism. I carried fear with me. I didn't want to take that home with me and impart it to my boys. So in March 2011 I resigned from my job at the CTD, and Anthony resigned from his job at the British Airport Authority. My colleagues were wonderful. They completely understood my decision to resign and, indeed, many of them were quite envious. Things were getting so difficult in the UK that many people were dreaming about escaping to warmer, brighter, sunnier climes in places like Australia.

My last day at work was very emotional. I had a wonderful send-off with great cards and presents from everyone there. I made a farewell speech, and noticed that some people were in tears. Within such a short period of time I'd forged a strong bond with men and women who were very special, and from whom I'd learnt a great deal.

Our building was on the South Bank, not far from Shakespeare's Globe, and it had great views of the Thames. This had been my norm: walking to work along London's celebrated river, past St Paul's Cathedral in the distance and Big Ben. For a girl from Perth, it was the stuff of dreams – or at least *my* dreams. I left the office for the last time – walked arm in arm with my colleagues along the Thames for the last time – and went on to have a fantastic farewell party at a very swanky bar above Shakespeare's Globe.

Hours later, leaving at the end of the night, I stared back at this part of London, which I will love all my life, and thought, *How lucky I've been – and how I'll miss all of this*. I hoped, too, that I'd played a small role in helping make our world a little safer, more just and tolerant, and more peaceful.

We left Britain on 29 April 2011, the day Prince William married Catherine Middleton. I'm a closet royalist when it comes to pomp and ceremony and had spent that morning glued to the TV, trying to ignore Anthony's entreaties for me to pack. The weather was glorious and there was a feeling of celebration in the air, with the Queen's Diamond Jubilee and the Olympics just around the corner. But we'd made our decision, and we had no regrets.

As we flew out of London I thought about fate, and how difficult it can be to find clarity in life when it comes to making decisions about the best direction to take. There was no doubt that Anthony and I had made the right decision to leave Britain, because it was time to put all our energy into three little lives and to build a safe future for them, just as I'd tried to contribute to building a safe future for the people of Iraq and the UK.

EPILOGUE

My days start early, as they always have. And it's just as well: with three boys who are manic from the second they open their eyes, I need to be up – not quite ready for battle, but ready for whatever they have in store for me and my husband. Each day rolls out much like a military operation; often I'll reflect on how useful my training in the army has been for civilian life. There are beds to be made, breakfasts to prepare, children to dress and organise. Anthony and I are a team in all of this, and we work together to manage our family.

The routine of each day helps me achieve all the things I need to do – and it helps me find the space for the things I *want* to do. When we arrive at kindergarten, I can take some time with my boys, to just be their mummy, to talk to their teachers and say hello to the other parents. When I can, I like to volunteer to cut up fruit for the children's morning tea, or take away some of the school washing that needs to be done.

When I arrive at work, I enter a male-dominated arena – I work for the Western Australian Police as an adviser to the commissioner. My official job title is 'counsel', but that doesn't really describe the breadth of work I do. This is a law enforcement agency where rank and men rule. Each day in my job is different. I could be appearing in court, and some times I only have a night, or a day or two, to prepare. If it's a big matter – a long trial – I may have already been preparing for a number of weeks. In an era of government cuts, my office is very under-resourced and underfunded, so I am the only lawyer at the agency's headquarters.

Invariably, before I go into court I've already had an opportunity to advise the commissioner of police on the matter; I will be very clear about what his instructions are and what is in the best interests of the agency, and if I've had any concerns prior to court I will have had the opportunity to express those. Ultimately my job is to be the voice of the agency and to follow instructions to a certain degree. Order and justice are still the themes of my work, and my life. I value order within a community, a society and a country as a path to justice. Partly what I feel I need to do in my work is to change the social order to better take care of the people who live within it – not to throw out that order, but keep the frameworks that already exist and mould them to accommodate different and progressive needs.

Part of my role as a senior lawyer is to advise and comment on policy and new legislation – that's a significant area where

I feel I can have some influence and some input. This is legislation that may affect human rights and the rights of children, for example. In that respect I continue to work on equality and social justice, and this balance between an individual's human and constitutional rights as opposed to maintaining law, order and peace in the community is always difficult to strike.

The work I am currently doing in the area of equality is twofold. I am involved in the drafting of equality and diversity policies within WA Police (including policies on gender transition in the workplace for transgender employees). On a personal level, I am endeavouring to challenge the outdated and sexist management attitudes towards working mothers, and those with other caring responsibilities, that seem to be still far too prevalent in the workforce today. While I have personally not experienced the full force of this form of sexism in my workplace, I have a number of close friends who are outstanding in their fields – professional women with years of training and experience behind them – who tell me stories about how having one child was tolerated, but by the time they had their second or third they were written off by the senior management in their companies as just being 'mummies'. These women had to leave their careers because they weren't being taken seriously any more. The injustice of this burns me. How can any society be equal when all of its citizens are not treated equally? How can any society truly be progressive if it does not value the contributions of *everyone* who is able to contribute, regardless of their sex or how many children they may happen to have? I am passionate about promoting flexible work practices as an efficient and successful business and human resources tool to promote the recruitment and, importantly, the retention of professional women. When I speak about women's issues and at women's groups, charities and in commercial settings, I talk about my journey not only for people who are interested in hearing it but as a vehicle to educate the community about equality, generally and in the workplace.

If given the opportunity in my career, I would in the future also like to address other equality issues, such as marriage equality, and address ethnic and cultural tensions in our community that have resulted from the recent influx of refugees and asylum seekers from North and East Africa and the Middle East, and the under-representation of indigenous and ethnic minority individuals in positions of senior management.

*

The underlying theme of my working days, though, is trying to make every minute of it count. I am a mother of small children and they are my priority. I try to be home before dinner most evenings. We are lucky to have help from Anthony's mother, who collects the boys from kindergarten. When I arrive home, they're normally very excited and rush to the door to give me a big hug. The boys tell me what they've been doing at kindergarten, talking over the top of each other with news. Then Anthony arrives home and we enter our evening phase of well-oiled machinery: making the boys their dinner, getting them into the bath and then into bed at about 8 pm. We physically can't manage to do it any earlier than that! The evening will often end with me falling asleep on the sofa in front of the TV or with a book in my lap, although quite often, after the boys go to bed, I'll prepare a matter for court the next day. Increasingly I am being asked to speak at functions, and then of course there was making time to write this book.

What never wavers in me is my sense of dedication to duty, whether it is duty to my job or duty to my family. I need both. And as a working mother, I can be committed to both parts of my life. I may not be perfect at everything but I can be committed to both. No one thing alone has to define any of us. My mission may have changed but the sense of mission persists. Equality and justice can be denied in all sorts of ways – and they need to be practised every single day. When I am prosecuting cases on behalf of the commissioner, I am trying to ensure that the law of the land is applied evenly and equally, and that where an injustice is done, it is corrected. It is not enough to talk about equality but then not take into account how fairness may include making provisions for workers to fulfil caring responsibilities, for example. I know that there are people – women, especially – who feel that they do not work in environments that practise equality and fairness, and they tell me that it is not acceptable. They say that it is something that all of us, women and men, need to work on together, and they are right.

It is all very well, of course, for me to say these things about equality – I have to live them too. Anthony and I have a true partnership in our house and in our marriage. I work one day a week from home and my husband works one day a week from home, too. There is no point in me giving speeches about equality and trying to work for justice in my job if my sons do not see it lived every day in their home.

I want my boys to grow up with all the survival skills. I want them to know how to cook, to wash, to fend for themselves – to be able to do things that have for so long been seen as women's domain. I want them to see men and women in an equal light, equally capable of great things and of doing whatever they want.

This is why we've made a conscious decision not to pressure our children into any religious following. We talk to them about all the religions in the world. We teach them that religion is a uniting concept, not a vehicle to divide, and that there are so many similarities between religions. It doesn't matter what religion, sexual orientation or skin colour you are, how you speak or where you come from – we're all different and we're all the same.

It is clearer to me now than ever before that the personal *is* political. Living what you believe every day is the most important thing to do. If you live your beliefs and morals every day, that is the substance of living a good life. It is not the easy path to take – it requires commitment and dedication. It also requires that you question yourself and test your beliefs, on a regular basis. But the alternative – to say that someone else should look after things for you, that someone else should just tell you what to do, say and believe – is to surrender agency in your own life.

I wake up every day knowing that I have forged my belief in justice and equality in the fire of all that has happened to me in my life. I didn't want to have to go to court to get equal justice served and that's not how I would have predicted things would end up, or how I would have liked my army career to end. But I have no regrets that I stood up and challenged the unjust, unfair and indefensible treatment directed at me. I remained true to my ideals and principles of equal and fair treatment, and social justice, and I can look at myself in the mirror knowing I was not a hypocrite. I used every ounce of courage and resolve I had to face what, at times, seemed to be insurmountable obstacles and challenges, and I knew when to walk away when more important issues (and lives) were at risk. I'm proud of how I lived up to my own values during that time.

I do not believe that any of the decisions made by the military or those in government were maliciously intended as personal attacks on me; rather, they were misguided or desperate attempts to downplay or conceal an incident that was perceived to have wider political ramifications – and I was simply the wrong person in the wrong situation at the wrong time to some extent.

The whole experience taught me humility, gave me courage and strength, inspired and motivated others to take action, influenced and paved the way for important changes within the armed forces, and reinforced something I have always been committed to: the idea that justice will be done and can be served, despite the odds.

I have learnt that I am an incredibly strong and resilient person who always strives for the truth and for authentic relationships, that I am someone whose principles, integrity and honesty are everything to them, someone who holds themselves and others to the highest standards, someone who truly needed and benefitted from the support of someone in my corner fighting alongside me: my husband. That was a feeling I hadn't really enjoyed or experienced before.

I have also learnt that I am a person who is prepared to lead the way and navigate uncharted waters for those that will later follow. I am a leader, not a follower, and I cannot remain in a community or environment where the actions of those around me are at odds with my principles and what I hold as sacred.

I will tell my sons the whole truth about the Jamiat affair. They need to know that their mother is human and fallible, but that she was willing to take a stand to ensure that changes were made for the better. I will teach them the importance of tolerance and forgiveness but also to be true to one's self and one's principles and to have a sense of fairness and justice. I will teach them not to be afraid to challenge concepts and behaviour, but to do so in a measured and respectful manner, with humility and a genuine desire to learn and understand.

Ultimately, I do not know how to live if I am not treating others equally – and also expecting the same of them. Equality – and the justice that must be applied in order to achieve it – is some of the hardest work we will undertake as human societies. But it's the most important.

Until we all believe that everyone else has the same rights as us, and we all work towards making that a reality, we are not truly human. It is only when every person on this planet can engage with every other person on this planet in a way that respects the other's inherent worth as a human being that we will have equality. This is not an easy thing to do – there are many people who do not want to believe we are all worthy of the same respect, even rights, as others. It is those people – not the people who show us the best of themselves – who really test our ability to believe in equality and justice. Those people, and the circumstances in which we encounter them, give us the opportunity to test our own beliefs and principles. That is a valuable lesson, and a gift, in its own way. It is the lesson I have learnt, and I am grateful for it.

ACKNOWLEDGEMENTS

Thank you so much to my husband Anthony, for his endless support, encouragement and enthusiasm. Thank you to my precious sons Aaron, Noah and Oscar, my raison d'etre and the lights in my life. I love and adore you with all my heart.

Thank you to Alan Lindsay for sewing the seed for this book. A big thank you to my agent Sophie Hamley for her belief, passion and hard work, and to everyone at Cameron Cresswell. My sincere gratitude to Nikki Barrowclough for finding the words when I couldn't. My appreciation also to Tom Gilliatt, Samantha Sainsbury and all at Pan Macmillan for their efforts and for having confidence in me.

My grateful acknowledgement of all the incredible women and men, both in my life and throughout history, who have enlightened and strengthened me.

Finally my thanks to all of you who have taken the time to read this book. I hope in some small way it resonates and perhaps inspires, motivates or empowers you. If so, it has all been worthwhile.